# BASEBALL
## THE PRESIDENTS' GAME

# BASEBALL
## THE PRESIDENTS' GAME

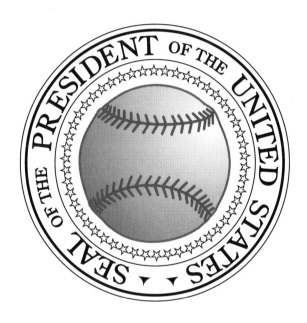

WILLIAM B. MEAD AND PAUL DICKSON

WALKER AND COMPANY
NEW YORK

Originally published in hardcover by Farragut Publishing Company in 1993; first paperback edition published in 1997 by Walker Publishing Company, Inc.

Published simultaneously in Canada by Thomas Allen & Son Canada, Limited, Markham, Ontario

Library of Congress Cataloging-in-Publication Data
Mead, William B.
Baseball: the presidents' game / William B. Mead and Paul Dickson.
p. cm.
Originally published: Washington, D.C.: Farragut Pub. Co., © 1993.
Includes bibliographical references (p. ) and index.
ISBN 0-8027-7515-2 (pbk.)
1. Baseball—Political aspects—United States. 2. Presidents—United States—Sports. 3. Sports and state—United States.
I. Dickson, Paul. II. Title.
[GV867.3.M43 1997]
796.357'0973—dc21 96-49052 CIP

Book design by Barkin & Davis, Inc.

Printed in the United States of America

2 4 6 8 10 9 7 5 3 1

OTHER BASEBALL BOOKS BY THE AUTHORS

**By William B. Mead**

*Baseball Goes to War* (Originally issued as *Even the Browns*)

*The Official New York Yankees Hater's Handbook*

*Two Spectacular Seasons*

*The Explosive Sixties*

*Low and Outside*

*The Inside Game*

**By Paul Dickson**

*The Dickson Baseball Dictionary*

*Baseball's Greatest Quotations*

# BASEBALL
# THE PRESIDENTS' GAME

1

# Opener

**W**ith the exception of Rutherford B. Hayes, who seemed preoccupied with croquet, every American president from George Washington on has had some link with baseball or baseball under one of its earlier names. Not all of them liked the game — a couple of them even disliked it — but for more than a century they have jumped at the opportunity to associate themselves with what has come to be known as the "national pastime." They savored the political benefits while recognizing the political costs should they dare to ignore baseball and its millions of fans.

The game played at Valley Forge by Washington's troops was almost certainly "rounders," an English antecedent of baseball, and the game played by John Adams as a boy was probably "one old cat." Abraham Lincoln played a variant of baseball in Illinois as well as in Washington. All these games involved a ball pitched by one player and hit by another, who ran to or around bases while the pitcher's teammates tried to catch the ball or otherwise put the batter out. Some may have been closer to cricket than to baseball, as we know the game today.

By 1857 some Americans were already beginning to call baseball the national pastime. During the Civil War baseball was played in army encampments on both sides. But it wasn't until after the war that baseball truly became what President Andrew Johnson called "the national game" — the most widely played sport in America. Baseball grew so popular that it was not until well after World War II that any other professional team sport came remotely close to matching it in terms of a mass following.

The national pastime is something presidents of the United States like to publicly embrace, and baseball is always eager to hug back. Nowadays world champions and aging stars are invited to the White House, leaving jerseys, baseball caps and television footage in their wakes. People may consider this part of modern political theater, but it goes back a long way. Big-league teams have been honored at the White House at least as far back as April 13, 1883, when President Chester A. Arthur greeted the Cleveland Forest Citys of the National League and declared that "good ballplayers make good citizens." Before that — before there were professionals — President Andrew Johnson hosted three teams at the White House.

Throwing out the first ball of the baseball season is an unwritten and valuable fringe benefit that comes with the job of American president. Politically, he wins no matter how weak his arm or how wild his throw. No king or dictator could create such a lofty yet playful role in a joyous setting of innocent springtime celebration. News photographers have been capturing the ritual since it began April 14, 1910, when William Howard Taft rose from the broad, sturdy chair that had been installed to accommodate his corpulent frame and hurled a ceremonial sphere to Washington's starting pitcher, the great Walter Johnson. In 1992 President George Bush carried on the tradition in Baltimore on Opening Day but lost his starting role for 1993 when he was beaten out by a young southpaw from Arkansas named Bill Clinton.

Granted, presidents, being politicians, come out to the ballpark for reasons besides a love of the game. Throwing out the first ball on Opening Day is a photo opportunity that will land his picture in virtually every newspaper in the country and on all of the television networks. Money can't buy that kind of non-controversial prominence. But more presidents that one would imagine have felt a genuine fondness for the game, a fondness that has gone well beyond self-interest.

George Bush was only the latest of many presidents with a lifelong attachment to baseball. Throughout his presidency, the old Yale first baseman kept his mitt, oiled and ready, in a desk drawer in the Oval Office. Other chief executives demonstrated their affection for the game in less direct ways. Richard Nixon devoured the history and records of baseball. Woodrow Wilson loved watching it. In the last, painful years of his life, one of his few remaining pleasures was being driven to Griffith Stadium where he would watch the game from his sedan, parked in the Senators' bullpen. There he was protected from foul balls and entertained by the likes of pitcher Al Schacht, who in time would become known as the Clown Prince of Baseball.

The Wilson story has become part of baseball lore. Because it is the national pastime, baseball is a great collector of lore — as well as myth. Just as some of the lore includes presidents, so do some of the myths. There is, for example, the supposed telephone call that FDR placed to Joseph Stalin one day during World War II. "Hello Joe, it's Frank. Giants three, Dodgers nothing." There are also equally delightful baseball myths involving Lincoln on his deathbed, Lincoln receiving word of his nomination to be president and a young Taft's potential as a pitching star.

Although presidents have benefited politically from their association with the sport, baseball hasn't fared badly from the relationship either. Presidential involvement in ceremonial baseball occasions boosts the game's standing — as well as paid attendance and television ratings. More specifically, baseball has enjoyed a certain largess from the U.S. government.

In 1922 the Supreme Court concluded, against all logic, that professional baseball was a game, not a business, and that professional baseball teams were not engaged in interstate commerce. Therefore, the court ruled, professional baseball clubs were not subject to antitrust laws. That judgment was affirmed a half-century later by the Supreme Court in an opinion by Justice Harry Blackmun that was based more on a sentimental love for baseball than on legal reasoning. Consequently, no other professional sport enjoys the nearly blanket exemption from antitrust laws that baseball does. At the outset of World War II key baseball figures lobbied behind the scenes to win from Franklin Roosevelt a letter to the commissioner of baseball encouraging the major leagues to continue playing during the war. FDR didn't write to the leaders of any other sport, and nobody wondered why.

No other sport has been so graced by presidential attention. Presidents don't pass out the first football, toss up the first basketball or tee up the first golf ball. Baseball, like the president, stands alone.

## TALKIN' BASEBALL

■ Ever since Franklin Roosevelt, presidents have often turned to baseball to get their point across. FDR and his speechwriters were masters at knowing how to communicate with the American public. They found baseball metaphors ideal and Roosevelt frequently employed them. In May 1933, two months after taking office, Roosevelt included the following in a radio address:

"I have no expectation of making a hit every time I come to bat. What I seek is the highest possible batting average, not only for myself, but for my team ...."

5

**LINCOLN CARTOONED**

This 1860 Currier and Ives cartoon shows Lincoln in a baseball setting, getting the better of rivals for the presidency: John Bell, John Breckinridge and Stephen Douglas. Lincoln was well-known to be a baseball fan.

# CHAPTER I

# The Fathers of the Tradition

*George Washington and his troops played at Valley Forge, Abraham Lincoln ran the bases with his coattails flying, and William McKinley passed up a chance to make presidential history.*

O n April 7, 1778, at Valley Forge, a Revolutionary War soldier named George Ewing wrote in his journal that during free time, he "played base." It is the first written reference to baseball in America, and it occurred under the managership, so to speak, of General George Washington.

Of Washington himself, an American soldier at Valley Forge wrote that "he sometimes throws and catches a ball for hours with his aide-de-camp." Washington and his troops probably were playing rounders, the British game that evolved into baseball.

John Adams, our second president, recalled his sporting youth in a letter written to Dr. Benjamin West, a prominent Philadelphian. Adams wrote that he spent his "mornings, noons and nights,

**WALL OF FAME**

At the beginning of the 1949 season, Clark Griffith points with subdued pride to his collection of photos of U.S. presidents throwing out the opening ball at Griffith Stadium. Griffith, for many decades the primary link between baseball and the presidency, may have made up some of the legends touting the presidents' baseball prowess.

making and sailing boats, in swimming, in skating, flying kites and shooting, in marbles, ninepins, bat and ball, football, quoits, and wrestling."

Thomas Jefferson, president No. 3, expressed a negative view. "Games played with the ball, and others of that nature, are too violent for the body and stamp no character on the mind," he wrote in a letter to one Peter Carr dated August 19, 1785. Jefferson's opinion was shared by many in the ruling class. Princeton College banned "baste ball," a popular game among students, on grounds that it "is in itself low and unbecoming gentlemen Students and ... is an exercise attended with great danger."

But American boys kept playing, and some of them became presidents. Andrew Jackson, like Adams, played "one old cat" or some other early version of baseball, and there are similarly firm but fragmentary mentions of the game in the papers of and about our other early presidents. This was not remarkable in a country that imported British traditions. In 1748, Mary Lepell, a member of the royal household, wrote that the Prince of Wales and his family "[entertain] themselves at baseball, a play all who are or have been schoolboys are well acquainted with."

America's early baseball, presidents included, vanished from historical reckoning because baseball chauvinistically decided, after the fact, to pretend that the game was invented out of the blue right here in America, and not until 1839. The mastermind of this historical revision was Albert Goodwill Spalding, a great pitcher in the earliest days of professional baseball, a founder of the National League, the president of the Chicago White Stockings and the founder of the sporting goods company that still bears his name.

Seeking export markets for his sporting goods, Spalding took a group of American baseball players on a worldwide tour. They returned in April 1889 to a heroes' welcome in New York, where they were feted at a banquet. The speakers included Mark Twain, who called baseball "the very symbol, the outward and visible expression of the drive and push and rush and struggle of the raging, tearing, booming nineteenth century." No president could have said it better.

Baseball, then as now, aroused waves of patriotism among the diners, and A.G. Mills, president of the National League, stood to tell the celebrants that baseball was not British after all, but purely American in origin. The audience loved it. "No rounders!" they chanted. "No rounders! No rounders!"

But Henry Chadwick, the most prominent sportswriter of the 19th century and the inventor of the box score, continued to write that baseball evolved from the British game of rounders.

The degree to which baseball and rounders are alike is well-documented. Rounders featured four bases positioned in a diamond. A feeder threw the ball to a striker who tried to hit the ball to score runs. The striker was out when he missed three tosses, batted a ball caught on the fly or was hit with a thrown ball while running the bases. If getting the runner out by hitting him with the ball sounds like a major deviation, it was a feature of some early forms of baseball, including the so-called Massachusetts game. One old cat was another link in the evolutionary chain.

Spalding was offended by this "rounders pap," and at his behest a commission was appointed to study the issue. A.G. Mills, he of "no rounders!" fame, was chairman. On December 30, 1907, after three years of slight study, the commission reported this conclusion:

"The first scheme for playing baseball, according to the best evidence obtainable to date, was devised by Abner Doubleday at Cooperstown, New York, in 1839." Let it be noted that Martin Van Buren was president in 1839 and that he knew of baseball but almost surely not of Abner Doubleday, who was a West Point plebe at the time he supposedly was devising a game of native pastoral beauty some hundred miles from the drill fields of the military academy.

A believer in the Doubleday myth, if any remain, would tell you that George Washington may have played rounders and John Adams may have played some kind of game, but neither could have played baseball, no way, because the game didn't exist back then.

Myths cloud other links between baseball and presidents as well. Two of the best center on Abraham Lincoln, one at the start of his presidential career and one at the end.

When Republicans convened in Chicago to choose their presidential candidate in 1860, Lincoln, a front-runner, waited in Springfield, Illinois. According to legend, he was playing baseball — or town ball, yet another ancestor of the game — when a delegation of bearded Republican elders arrived to tell him that his GOP brethren had chosen him as their standard bearer. "I am glad to hear of their coming," Lincoln supposedly said, "but they will have to wait a few minutes while I have another turn at bat."

Lincoln did, in fact, play ball in Springfield, but more credible accounts of that particular day place him at the Springfield railroad depot with his ear to the telegraph line from Chicago.

The other Lincoln myth is a true whopper, aired as if real by radio sportscaster Bill Stern in the 1940s: As Lincoln lay near death, he beckoned General Abner Doubleday to his side. "Abner," whispered the Great Emancipator with his dying breath, "don't let baseball die."

Poor Doubleday never asked for these phantom roles. He was a real person, in fact a real Union general, and he is buried beneath an elaborate memorial at Arlington National Cemetery. But his alleged connection with baseball is false. Indeed, there is no evidence that he ever played the game. Nor was he around when Lincoln died.

Baseball didn't need to mythologize Lincoln, because the Railsplitter really did play the game. Lincoln's interest in baseball is well-documented. He even played while in the White House. An account of Lincoln playing baseball with youngsters was passed down by a grandson of Francis Preston Blair, a confidant of presidents and one-time owner of Blair House, the mansion across the street from the White House which now accommodates presidential guests.

"We boys hailed his coming with delight," the young man wrote, "because he would always join us ... on the lawn. I remember vividly how he ran, how long were his strides, how far his coattails stuck out behind .... "

Lincoln occasionally strolled out behind the White House to watch a few innings of baseball on the White Lot, which extended from the back of the White House to the Washington Monument. Most of that area is now a park called the Ellipse, where the national Christmas tree is erected each year.

Baseball was then going through local permutations. New Englanders played the Massachusetts game, New Yorkers played the New York game and Washingtonians played the Washington game. The Washington game's rules produced astronomical scores. There were no outfield fences, and a batter who hit the ball far enough could keep running around and around the bases. In 1866, a year after Andrew Johnson succeeded Lincoln as president, Washington beat Richmond on one memorable occasion by a score of 102-87. The National Baseball Association, an amateur league that played on the White Lot, left records displaying a record score of 211-189 — an even 400 runs. It was a case of evolution lurching backwards, because the rounders played at Washington's Valley Forge was much closer to modern baseball than the game watched by Lincoln on the White Lot.

Lincoln may not have whispered to Doubleday, but he did leave the White House in the hands of a real baseball fan. President Andrew Johnson, too, watched games on the White Lot, including one that somehow matched three teams. According to an account by I. Kirk Sale in *Sport* magazine, Johnson "became so caught up with the prospect of a two-inter city match between the Washington Nationals, Philadelphia Athletics and Brooklyn Atlantics that he gave government clerks and employees time off to watch." Sale added: "Andrew Johnson set the whole White House entourage up on plush straight-back chairs along the first-base line and that day became the first President to watch an inter-city baseball game." Johnson then invited the teams to the White House — another first.

**SULTAN AND PRINCE**
Babe Ruth signs a ball for their Imperial Highnesses, the Royal Prince and Princess Kaya of Japan, on August 15, 1934, at Yankee Stadium. Overseas VIPs often feel the same need to go to the ballpark as do American politicos.

In August 1867 the National Base Ball Club of Washington opened a new ballpark. Thousands attended the first game, and President Johnson was guest of honor, beaming from a special seat on the clubhouse balcony. A few weeks before he had accepted an honorary membership in the Mutual Club of New York, a baseball team sponsored by the Tammany Hall political machine.

The Johnson files at the National Archives in Washington include several offers of such honorary memberships. Typical was one from Frank Diamond Rogers of the Enterprise Baseball Club of Philadelphia. "As your lamented predecessor Abraham Lincoln, did not refuse the membership of a Fire Company," reasoned Rogers, "we hope you will not scorn this humble offer of a membership in our National Game, but, accept it as a token of our esteem for you as a man, our veneration as a patriot, and our admiration as a statesman."

(Many members of Congress did not share this high opinion of Johnson, a pugnacious Tennessean. He was embroiled in bitter conflict with members of his own party in Congress over policy for Reconstruction of the defeated South. This led to his impeachment by the House and trial by the Senate. He was acquitted by one vote in May 1868.)

At one White House gathering of supporters, Johnson reminisced about playing baseball as a boy, talked of the game's "moral" nature, and pronounced baseball the "national game" of the United States.

The contrast between Lincoln, who was more a baseball player, and Andrew Johnson, who was more a fan, reflected change in America. As the Industrial Revolution brought people to the cities, the rural pastime of baseball acquired a new dimension as an urban spectator sport. In Washington, games on the White Lot attracted big crowds, but the field was not enclosed and admission was free. The game Johnson attended in August 1867 was at a new, enclosed park, and tickets cost a quarter. George Wright, a renowned shortstop of the era, starred for the team, and was paid. Ballplayers were becoming celebrities, and celebrities always have been welcome at the White House.

In 1876 the National League was formed. Ulysses S. Grant, who as president watched games on the White Lot, watched the New York Gothams play their first game at the Polo Grounds East Diamond on May 1, 1883. John Troy, the Gotham shortstop, made five errors, but New York nevertheless beat Boston, 3-2.

Chester A. Arthur was president then, and was proud to host the Cleveland Forest Citys at the White House on April 13, 1883. "Good ballplayers make good citizens," the president said. When the New York Gothams came to Washington later that season, Arthur invited them in, too. As the players were presented to him, Arthur supposedly turned to the team's manager, Jim Mutrie, and said, "They're all giants, aren't they?" Legend has it that Arthur's comment prompted Mutrie to name his team the Giants. It is not true. Mutrie himself came up with the name. But it is a good presidential-baseball story.

Arthur was succeeded in office by Grover Cleveland, and the next team in the White House was Chicago. The great White Stockings team of Cap Anson dropped by in 1885. "How's my old friend Jimmy Galvin?" Cleveland asked Anson. "You know, he and I were good friends when I was a sheriff and mayor of Buffalo." Cleveland ran in fast company; Pud Galvin, "The Little Steam Engine," was a renowned player and manager of the era. He is in the Baseball Hall of Fame, alongside President Cleveland's namesake, the great pitcher Grover Cleveland Alexander — who, as you will read later in this book, was portrayed in a Hollywood movie by a future president named Ronald Reagan.

Anson locked President Cleveland in a powerhouse grip. Next in line was Mike (King) Kelly, the greatest baseball hero of his time. "There wasn't a man in the crowd that wasn't six feet in height and they were all in lovely condition," Kelly wrote of the visit. "Their hands were as hard as iron. The president's hand was fat and soft. I squeezed it so hard that he winced. Then George Gore did the same and Burns and Dalrymple did likewise. The president's right hand was almost

**CONGRESSIONAL CLASSIC**

Rep. Walter B. Huber (R-Ohio) sells Cracker Jack at the 1947 congressional baseball game at Griffith Stadium. The contest marked resumption of the Democratic and Republican rivalry after the interruption of World War II.

double in size and he was glad when it was all over. He would rather shake hands with 1,000 people than a ball nine after that day. He didn't shake hands with us again when we parted. He impressed me as being a charming, courteous gentleman who has considerable backbone, and democratic enough to be a Democratic president of our glorious country."

As the players left, Anson asked Cleveland to come out and see a game. "What do you imagine the American people would think of me if I wasted my time going to the ball game?" Cleveland replied, reflecting his stern sense of duty. Cleveland was no athlete; at 250 pounds he was our second-heaviest president. He once said that "bodily movement is among the dreary and unsatisfactory things of life." Staying away from the ballpark showed a commendable work ethic, but it was a political miscalculation: Cleveland was defeated in the next election by Benjamin Harrison, a Republican who knew better.

Cleveland showed his stuff and won a second term in 1892, becoming the only president to make such a comeback. Somewhat mellowed in his second term, he heard with enthusiasm young John Heydler's recitation of "Casey at the Bat." Heydler, then a government clerk, was called upon to recite while delivering a message to the White House. Years later he became president of the National League.

**ELDER STATESMEN**

Ty Cobb, late in his career, with William Jennings Bryan, late in his. Both men had been at the top of their games near the turn of the century, when Cobb led the Detroit Tigers to pennants in 1907, 1908 and 1909 and Bryan was the Democratic presidential nominee in 1896, 1900 and 1908.

Cobb, "the Georgia Peach," was a Southern Democrat in the old-fashioned sense. In 1912 he declared his support for Woodrow Wilson and in 1920 he publicly supported Democrat James M. Cox. Yet Cobb became friendly with Republican William Howard Taft, who defeated Bryan in the 1908 election. Taft and Cobb met at the White House in 1909. Taft liked to play golf at Augusta, Georgia, and once told Cobb that they were "fellow citizens" of Augusta. "The only difference is that down there they think you're a bigger man than I am," Taft added. Quite a turn of language for the 330-pound Taft. He and Cobb subsequently golfed together at Augusta several times.

A paunchy Hoosier known as the "human iceberg," Benjamin Harrison was respected for his intellect and honesty, if not his common touch. Nevertheless, on June 6, 1892, Harrison became the first president to attend a major league baseball game. He saw Cincinnati beat Washington 7-4 in 11 innings at the Swampoodle Grounds, a modestly named ballpark long since razed to accommodate Washington's Union Station. *Sporting Life*, a national baseball weekly of the period, noted the president's presence and said that he did not prove to be a mascot for the home team. Harrison returned to the Swampoodle Grounds June 25 and saw Washington succumb to Philadelphia, 9-2.

While Harrison was cheering for the Washington team, William McKinley was preparing for the presidency as governor of Ohio. He threw out the first ball of the season at Columbus in 1892 and Columbus went on to win the Western League championship. On April 19, 1897, just a few months after his inauguration, McKinley greeted the Washington Senators in the Oval Office. *Sporting Life* greeted the new president with this warm headline:

M'KINLEY ON BALL
THE PRESIDENT A LOVER OF THE NATIONAL GAME
The Washington Team Presented to the Nation's Chief Executive — He Speaks
Encouragingly of the Sport and Will Attend Many Games

Gus Schmelz, the Washington manager, had managed Columbus in 1892. He reminded McKinley that he had thrown out the first ball and that Columbus had proceeded to win the pennant. Opening Day in Washington was only five days ahead, and Schmelz suggested to the president that he throw out the first ball again, perhaps blessing the team with a championship omen.

According to *Sporting Life*, "The president smiled and replied that he remembered the incident very well, indeed, and that if he saw his way clear he would repeat the performance at National Park Thursday."

The Senators were not blind to the prestige a presidential appearance would impart. A presidential box was erected and adorned with flags and bunting. More than 100 members of the Senate and House showed up, but the president did not, as the Washington *Star* noted. "President McKinley disappointed the 7,000 spectators at the opening game by failing to appear, and the Senators disappointed them by losing to Brooklyn 5 to 4," the *Star* reported.

McKinley, who liked baseball, had missed a soft chance for real history. His successor, Theodore Roosevelt, was of another mind, and the initial first-ball glory would pass to William Howard Taft. But then, history is always a reminder of missed opportunities.

## THE RAPPAHANNOCK TOSS

■ In his 1800 biography of George Washington, Reverend Mason L. Weems created the most durable myths about the childhood of our first president: chopping down the cherry tree and throwing a silver dollar across the Rappahannock River.

In 1936 the city of Fredericksburg, Virginia, decided to honor Washington's 204th birthday by celebrating these fables. They planted 200 cherry trees and the governor of the Commonwealth invited the great pitcher Walter Johnson to come down from his Maryland retirement and attempt the silver dollar pitch on February 22.

Johnson accepted the challenge on the conditions that someone else furnish the dollar and that no one try to make him don colonial garb. Meanwhile, Congressman Sol Bloom of New York, director of the commission to celebrate the Washington Bicentennial, laid odds of 20-to-1 that Johnson, then 48 years old, could not throw the dollar to the other side of the river.

The 22nd was a cold day with ice in the river and snow on the banks, but that did not deter the crowd of 10,000. Johnson, in shirtsleeves, had three silver dollars. The first one missed, falling short of the 272 feet to the bank on the opposite shore. The second made it, and the third — the official dollar of the try — sailed across the river. The greatest right-handed pitcher in history had replicated the feat that Parson Weems had attributed to the 11-year-old George Washington.

**STAGED EVENT**
This unique vista shows photographers waiting for President Coolidge to throw the first ball to pitcher Walter Johnson on April 15, 1924. Opening Day has been a photo "op" (as in opportunity) for decades.

# CHAPTER II

# The Bully Baseball Baiter

*Teddy Roosevelt scorned baseball as a refuge for the middle-aged.*

t must have galled him. Here he was, a popular president renowned for his rough-and-tumble physical prowess, a former war hero who boxed for exercise. He publicly scorned non-bruising sports, baseball among them, as "mollycoddle games." Nevertheless, he was being used, manipulated, by the powers of baseball, a sport he considered too tame for red-blooded Americans.

But baseball was the national game, the national pastime. It wanted to embrace the president, to make him part of the mystique. How could he say no to a game that was becoming almost a national religion?

So here he was, in his office, on May 16, 1907, receiving a delegation from the National Association of Professional Base Ball Leagues, which pressed upon him a season pass that he would never use. John H. Farrell made the presentation with these words, among many others:

"To its devotees all over this fair land from ocean to ocean there is nothing more gratifying than the fact that the present executive head of this great nation is an ardent champion of the National Game. It is the pleasure of this committee ... to recognize your practical support of a game that nourishes no 'mollycoddles'.... We desire to make you one of us."

NATIONAL PORTRAIT GALLERY

**MOLLYCODDLE GAME**
Teddy Roosevelt boxed, wrestled, hunted big game and admired contact sports like football. Despite his misgivings, baseball seduced him.

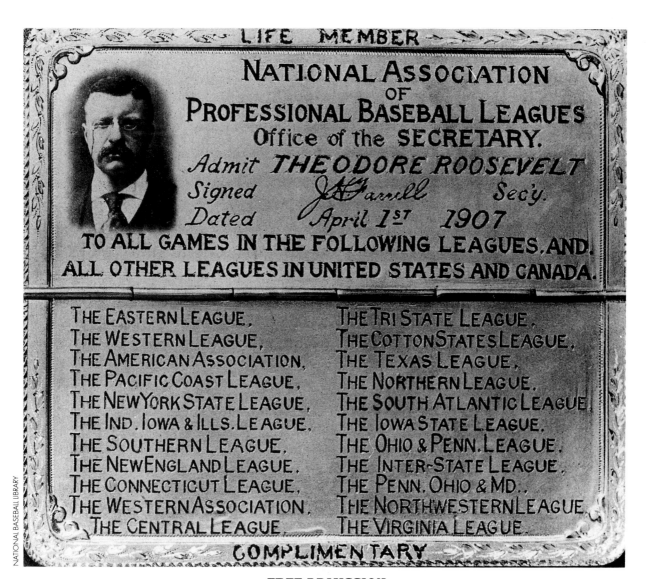

**FREE ADMISSION**

**One of baseball's master strokes of publicity is the annual presentation of a season pass to the president, who, of course, hardly needs it to get into a game. Here's the first one, presented to President Theodore Roosevelt on May 16, 1907. It was 14-karat gold, two pieces hinged together, with Roosevelt's likeness engraved in gold. This one admitted Teddy to 256 ballparks, most of them in the minor leagues.**

There. He had even turned Teddy's disdainful term, "mollycoddles," to baseball's advantage. The White House press corps was taking all of this in. Roosevelt had to respond. He did, damning the game with faint praise. A press account paraphrased Roosevelt's response this way:

"The president expressed his warm thanks for the beautiful gold card which was presented to him, and said that he regarded the game of base ball as the typical American outdoor sport; that he was particularly interested in the game because men of middle-age could still engage in it; that the game always had his good wishes, as had every outdoor sport."

They had him. The only president ever to express his dislike for baseball was co-opted. What's more, his sons Kermit and Quentin played baseball and enjoyed it. Roosevelt invited Kermit's schoolboy team to play a game on the White House grounds and was embarrassed for the losers after Kermit's team routed the opposing P Street Boys, 23-4. "It was all right," Kermit assured his father. "I filled them afterward with lemonade."

Could it be that Roosevelt's sons made a fan of him? "I like to see Quentin practicing baseball," the president wrote. "It gives me hope that one of my boys will not take after his father in this respect, and will prove able to play the national game."

In a letter to a third son, Archie, Roosevelt wrote this about Quentin, the son he was to lose in World War I: "Quentin really seems to be getting on pretty well with his baseball. In each of the last two games he made a base hit and a run."

Not that the old Rough Rider was thoroughly converted. In a more typical letter to Kermit, he wrote: "I do like to feel that you are manly and able to hold your own in rough, hardy sports .... I am glad you play football; I am glad that you box and ride and shoot and walk and row as well as you do."

In 1908, his last year as president, Roosevelt broke down completely and received two big-league teams in the White House. Manager Clark Griffith brought in his New York Highlanders (now the Yankees) on May 5 and Charles "Piano Legs" Hickman, a colorful player of the era, led in his fellow Cleveland Naps (now Indians) on May 27. According to *The New York Times*, Roosevelt told Griffith he would have "felt insulted" if the Highlanders hadn't dropped by. He said son Quentin was the family baseball expert, one who knew all the players and their averages.

## TEDDY THE UMP?

■ Grantland Rice, the renowned sportswriter and sports-page poet, suggested that Teddy Roosevelt would find umping a rough enough occupation after his tame White House years. Rice's poem, "A Tip To Teddy," appeared in *Baseball* magazine in 1909, shortly before Roosevelt's presidential term expired.

That's the only job for you, take your tip now, Theodore
Think of how your pulse will leap when you hear the
angry roar
Of the bleacher gods in rage, you will find the action there
Which you've hunted for in vain, in the Presidential chair.
Chasing mountain lions and such, catching grizzlies will
seem tame
Lined up with the jolt you'll get in the thick of some close
game.
Choking angry wolves to death as a sport will stack up raw
When you see Kid Elberfeld swinging for your under-jaw,
When you hear Hugh Jennings roar, "Call them strikes, you
lump of cheese!"
Or McGraw comes rushing in, kicking at your shins and
knees.

Roosevelt didn't know it, but in receiving Clark Griffith he planted the seed for decades of close kinship between baseball and the White House. Griffith became manager of the Washington Senators in 1912, mortgaged his ranch to buy the team, ran the Senators until his death in 1955 and cultivated every president from Teddy Roosevelt through Dwight Eisenhower.

CLEVELAND PUBLIC LIBRARY

**FLAG DAY**
The largest flag in the world, circa 1937, is displayed on Flag Day in the Griffith Stadium outfield. The stadium's location in Washington made it a showplace for patriotic themes.

*"Father and all of us regarded baseball as a mollycoddle game. Tennis, football, lacrosse, boxing, polo, yes: They are violent, which appealed to us. But baseball? Father wouldn't watch it, not even at Harvard!"*

— Alice Roosevelt Longworth, daughter of Teddy Roosevelt

**GOOD PEG**
President Taft uncorking a belated ball to celebrate the 1912 season. He missed the opener when concerns about the *Titanic* disaster kept him at the White House. But the new Washington Senators owner, Clark Griffith, hoping to establish an annual event, asked Taft to throw out a symbolic first ball later in the season. Taft did so on June 18th, during a 17-game Washington winning streak.

# CHAPTER III

# The Biggest Booster

*When William Howard Taft threw out the first ball of the 1910 season, he established an unbreakable link between the presidency and baseball.*

**M**ajor Archie Butt, the popular gent who served as military aide to presidents Theodore Roosevelt and William Howard Taft, was the man who got Taft out of the White House and over to the ballpark. "I thought it would be just as necessary to get his mind off business as it was to exercise," Butt recalled in his memoirs.

What's more, he had a pass. On April 8, 1909 Thomas C. Noyes of the Washington Senators dropped by to give a season pass to Taft and another to Vice President James S. Sherman. The passes were handsome articles in Russian leather card cases with monograms embossed in heavy gold letters on the inside. Noyes encouraged Taft to come on over and see a game.

After much prodding by Butt, Taft agreed that he would enjoy such an outing and the date of April 19, 1909, was set to make him the first president since Harrison to attend a major league ball game. Butt and Senators' owner Tom Noyes went out early that day to select a box and purchase an extra-large chair for the nearly 300-pound president to sit in.

**FIRST SHOWING**
**William Howard Taft at the ballpark, with Vice President Sherman to his right. This is the first known photograph of a president at the ballpark, dated May 5, 1909.**

23

"One loves him at first sight," was Teddy Roosevelt's envious assessment of Taft, and his first entrance into the ballpark underscored the point. He came late — in formal tails and a top hat — and the next morning's *Washington Post* reported, "The game was interrupted by the cheering, which spread in a great wave from the grandstand to the bleachers as the crowd recognized the president."

Taft loved it. He stayed to the bitter end and ducked as foul balls shot back to his unscreened box. He shared nickel bags of peanuts with the vice president and expressed concern over the crowds' disputing of several calls. Butt puckishly reassured him: "They never kill the umpire before the seventh inning."

The presidential party watched the Nats get beaten by the Red Sox, 8-4. In 1925 Walter Johnson recalled the day in his serialized memoirs for the *Washington Times*: "I'll never forget the first time President Taft appeared at our ball park ... in the season of 1909 and our players got so excited that we 'booted' the game away to the Red Sox." Taft sensed that he might be having an impact on the game, turning to Butt as the Sox took a 6-0 lead and remarking, "I hope I am not a hoodoo."

That was Taft's first day at the ballpark as president. His most memorable occurred the following spring, on April 14, 1910. It was Opening Day for the Washington Senators, and the day began badly for Taft. Suffragists were then pressing the notion that women be allowed to vote. At 9:30 a.m. the president addressed their convention, and cautioned "the least desirable persons" might exercise power if women were given the vote.

As reported in *The Washington Post*, "This did not please the suffragists, and although President Taft was their guest, his speech was interrupted by an outburst of hisses from all over the hall. With the hisses were half-suppressed 'catcalls.' It was a trying moment for the president and for the national officers of the suffragist association who surrounded him on the platform. Expressions of alarm spread over the countenances of those on the rostrum and of many in the crowded hall.

"President Taft's color heightened but he did not lose his poise. Resuming his speech, he said:

'Now, my dear ladies, you must show yourselves equal to self-government by exercising, by listening to opposing arguments, that degree of restraint without which successful self-government is impossible.'

"At the conclusion of his talk he was enthusiastically applauded."

That afternoon, the president made his grand entrance to American League Park. Ban Johnson, president of the American League, had invited Taft to throw out the opening ball, and the president was ready. Mrs. Taft held the ball while the president removed his new kid gloves. He then took the ball and threw it to Washington's Opening Day pitcher, Walter Johnson. Taft's throw, like those of most presidents to follow, was not very good, but Johnson managed to reach down and catch it.

All this took place without advance publicity. That morning *The Washington Post* had reported that "the opening will not be attended by any ceremony." Yet it was the first time a president had thrown out the first ball of a baseball season. Photographers were on hand, and the next day's sports pages were dominated by the large, photogenic president. Johnson kept the ball and asked a friend to take it to the White House the next day and ask Taft to sign it. Taft did so, with a flourish. "To Walter Johnson," he wrote, "with the hope that he may continue to be as formidable as in yesterday's game. William H. Taft."

The effect of Taft's throw was indelible. Once and forever it wrapped the flag and the president around the game. Since Taft began the custom, every president except Jimmy Carter has made at least one such appearance.

The 1910 game was also the first opening game at which movies were made. The lone cameraman scored a cinematic scoop, enabling many more than the 15,000 at the game to see the historic first toss.

## ENDORSEMENTS

■ William Howard Taft loved to endorse baseball and maybe the most bullish example came on May 4, 1910, in a St. Louis speech.

"The game of baseball is a clean straight game, and it summons to its presence everybody who enjoys clean, straight athletics," he declared. "It furnishes amusement to the thousands and thousands. And I like it for two reasons — first, because I enjoy it myself and second, because if by the presence of the temporary chief magistrate such a healthy amusement can be encouraged, I want to encourage it."

Quite coincidentally, 1910 was also a good year for other baseball traditions. Jack Norworth's song "Take Me Out to the Ball Game" swept the country to become the game's anthem.

The opener also turned out to be a helluva ball game. Walter Johnson, perhaps the greatest pitcher in baseball history, was pitching the first of 13 openers in a row for the Senators. He shut out the Philadelphia Athletics 3-0 on one hit, and a very cheap hit at that. It was customary back then for overflow crowds to stand behind ropes in the outfield, and a fly ball by Frank "Home Run" Baker dropped for a double when right fielder Doc Gessler, backing up to catch the ball, tripped over the feet of an uncooperative fan.

In another time at bat, Baker inadvertently frightened the fans by hitting a foul ball that glanced off the head of Secretary of the Senate Charles G. Bennett. Unhurt, he waved off assistance and reassured the throng.

After that opener, Taft became one of baseball's most inexhaustible promoters. This is how his role as First Fan was described in the 1911 *Spalding's Official Base Ball Guide*: "President Taft believes in Base Ball.... He tells his friends that it is a pastime worth every man's while and advises them to banish the blues by going to a ball game and waking up with the enthusiasts of the bleachers who permit no man to be grouchy among them."

The players and fans loved him. Walter Johnson and Taft seemed to have a mutual admiration society. So did Taft and Ty Cobb, the fierce star of the Detroit Tigers. Taft tried to see Cobb play as often as his schedule permitted and *The Washington Post's* J.B. Grillo reported in 1911 that "the Detroit club never comes to Washington that Cobb does not make a visit to the White House."

Taft had many other great baseball days. On May 4, 1910, he became the only president to see games in each major league on the same day. It took place in St. Louis, where he sat through the first two innings of a game featuring his hometown Cincinnati team playing the Cardinals at National League Park. With the Cardinals already leading 12-0, he decided to leave the game and rush across town to Sportsman's Park where the great Cy Young was pitching

*Opposite page:*
**HISTORIC MOMENT**
**President Taft throwing out the first "first ball," on April 19, 1910, creating an American ritual of spring. In his book, *The Washington Senators*, Morris A. Bealle said that "President Taft, in spite of a big bay window, threw the ball with the finesse and grace of an accomplished ball player. ... His successors, Wilson, Harding, Coolidge, Hoover and Roosevelt, all used the bean-bag stance of a bloomer girl debutante."**

25

## WAS PRESIDENT TAFT A FRUSTRATED BALLPLAYER?

■ One of baseball's hoariest and phoniest legends is that William Howard Taft almost played big-league baseball himself. Clark Griffith liked to tell the story, and may have made it up himself.

Anyone looking at Taft would assume he could function only as a backstop. In fact, he was an avid player as a boy, and a power hitter, but because of his size he was a poor base runner.

But the story told by sportscaster Bill Stern in the late 1940s portrayed Taft as a promising young catcher offered a contract with the Cincinnati Red Stockings. He decided to accept despite the vehement objections of his father. But tragedy struck. In his last game before becoming a pro, young Bill wrecked his arm and his career was over before it began. Nothing left but to go to Yale, join Skull and Bones, become a lawyer, a judge, president of the United States and chief justice of the Supreme Court.

A second Taft myth had him inadvertently creating the seventh-inning stretch. In this yarn, the president traveled to Pittsburgh and attended a ball game in 1910. In the seventh inning, he got up to move his large body. The crowd, thinking that he was leaving the park, rose to their feet in respect. Taft sat back down and — voila — the seventh-inning stretch.

Nice, but untrue. More than forty years earlier, in 1869, Harry Wright of the Red Stockings wrote to a friend about a local custom: "The spectators all arise between halves of the seventh inning, extend their legs and arms and sometimes walk about. In so doing they enjoy the relief afforded by relaxation from a long posture on hard benches."

for Cleveland against the Browns. *The Sporting News* described the feat as "one of the most amazing days the sport ever enjoyed."

Taft showed up again for the 1911 opener in Washington, but missed in 1912, sending Vice President Sherman in his place. The *Titanic* had struck an iceberg and sank on April 15, four days before Opening Day. The death toll reached 1,595, among them Archie Butt, the convivial aide who first persuaded Taft to attend a ball game. The president was too busy with the disaster and too depressed by the loss of friends to play the happy leader at a ball game.

Clark Griffith, a turn-of-the-century pitching star turned baseball entrepreneur, had just taken over the Senators, and was determined to make the presidential first ball an annual event that would inspire the populace, reflect sunshine on America and sell tickets. So he announced an after-the-fact opening day of June 18, 1912. Taft accepted and it turned out to be the most glorious day in the early history of the Washington franchise.

The dreadful Senators had made a run from last place to second by winning 16 games in a row. A record crowd showed up and ticket scalpers were getting $5 for a dollar seat and $50 for a box. Congress adjourned early, businesses shut down at noon and the record crowd of 15,516 went wild when Taft and Sherman arrived. Taft waved his hat at the beginning of the game and Sherman threw his in the air at the end. As Joe Jackson, sports editor of *The Washington Post*, described the contest, the home team "made one of those 'story book' ninth-inning finishes and defeated the world champion Athletics by a score of 5 to 4 bringing their string of successive victories up to 17 replete with sensations."

Taft must have enjoyed the respite from his embattled presidency. He had broken with his friend and patron Theodore Roosevelt, who had declared his candidacy for president and would

**AT THE PARK**

**President Taft at Forbes Field, Pittsburgh, for the first National Mine Safety Demonstration, October 31, 1911. Taft wouldn't miss any event at a ballpark, even if it had nothing to do with baseball.**

ultimately run as candidate for the Progressive (Bull Moose) Party. Roosevelt and Taft split the Republican vote in the election of 1912, and Democrat Woodrow Wilson was elected.

The first-ball custom re-established, there has been no thought of giving it up. Later in 1912 Griffith prevailed on Ban Johnson, president of the American League, to allow the Senators a home opener every year because of the showcase it gave the game. Griffith embraced the custom to the point where he claimed decades later to have started it. "I inaugurated the custom back in 1912, when William Howard Taft was in office," he boasted in a 1955 *This Week* article immodestly titled "Presidents who Have Pitched for Me."

Griffith was conveniently forgetting 1910, when he was managing in faraway Cincinnati and President Taft threw out the season's first ball in Washington. Griffith had many accomplices in linking the office of president to baseball, but the first and most willing was President Taft.

**HISTORIC SHAKE**
Taft and Clark Griffith shake at the belated 1912 presidential opener. The Senators beat the Athletics 5-4.

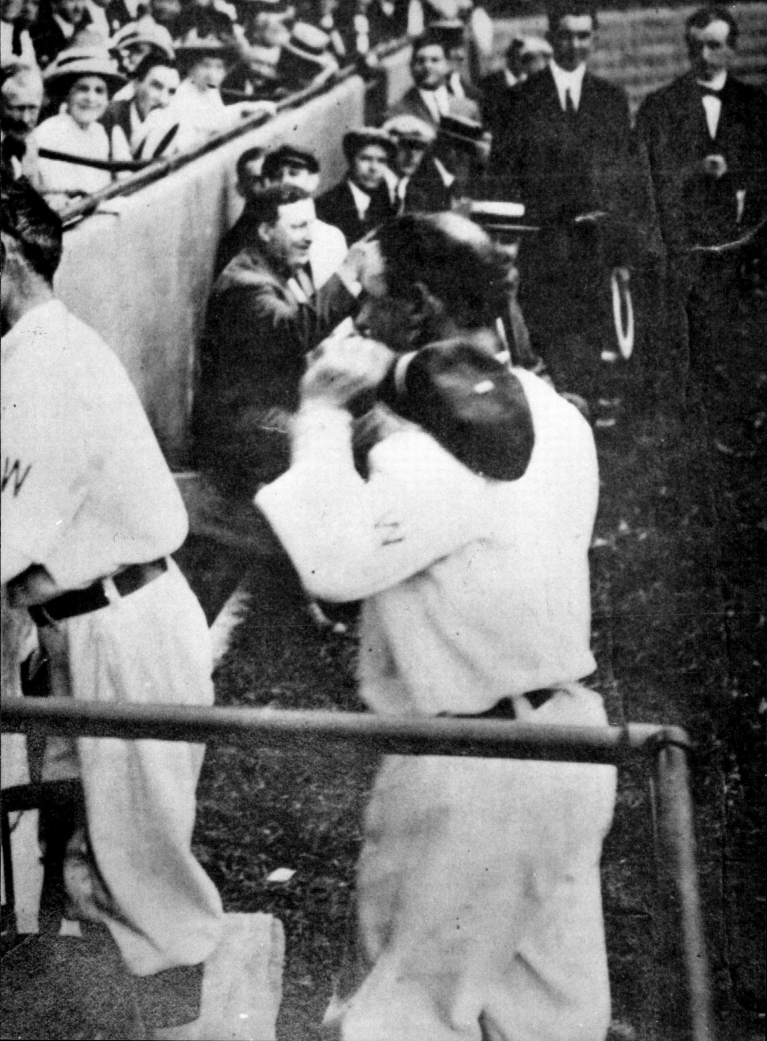

## CHAPTER IV
# The Scholar-Athlete

*In the last years of his life, Woodrow Wilson remained an ardent fan.*

President Woodrow Wilson played freshman baseball at Davidson College and enthusiastically threw out opening-day balls for a game he truly loved. He was the man to fuse the practice into the game's package of traditions. Even before the first opener he tipped *The Sporting News* to the fact that he would be a frequent visitor to American League Park in Washington. He added that he intended to be a "paying fan" rather than a "dead head" and not make use of the passes which would be presented to him.

The fans were starting to go to Opening Day expecting to see the president, and Wilson did not disappoint during his first spring in office. "Every neck was craned to glimpse the 'first American' as he rose to toss the ball to Walter Johnson, by every true Washingtonian thought to

LIBRARY OF CONGRESS

### HERE IT COMES
**President Wilson sends one out at the 1916 opener, while to his right Mrs. Wilson delights in the spectacle.**

31

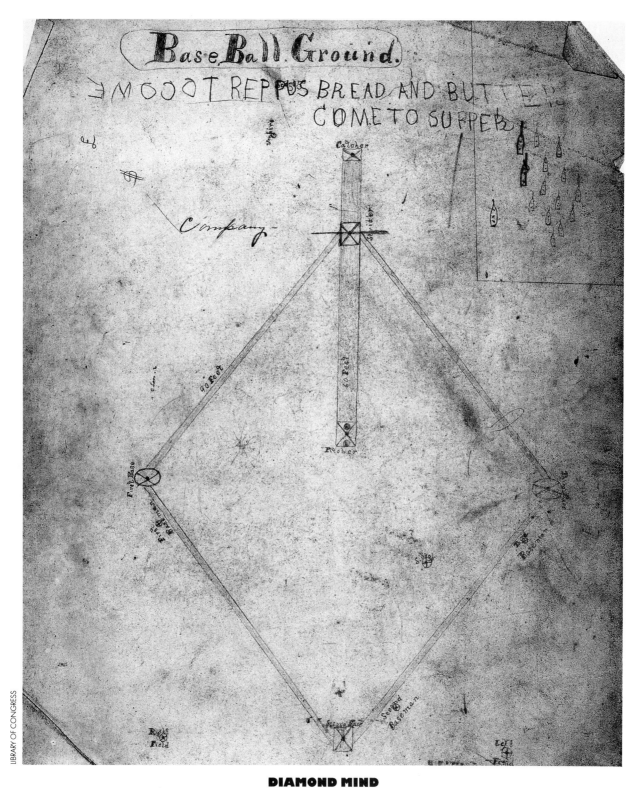

## DIAMOND MIND

**A page from Woodrow Wilson's boyhood notebook, demonstrating that baseball figured prominently in his life from an early age.**

## ENGAGEMENT PARTY

In their first public appearance since announcing their engagement, President Wilson appeared with Edith Galt on October 15, 1915, at the second game of the World Series in Philadelphia. Wilson, the first president to attend a World Series, insisted on paying for his own tickets. The Red Sox evened the series by beating the Phillies 2-1.

be the 'first pitcher.' Johnson had already received several ovations but as he caught the ball from the President's hand men and women arose that they might make more vociferous their tribute to the hero of the diamond."

Wilson made it to two of the next three openers and on all occasions the Senators won the game. Because war had just been declared, he missed the 1917 opener and the Nats lost in the 13th inning. The 1917 opener was interesting for another reason; before Vice President Thomas R. Marshall — the man who is still remembered as the author of the line "What this country really needs is a good five-cent cigar" — threw out the first ball, there was a flag ceremony where Griffith and the young assistant secretary of the Navy, Franklin D. Roosevelt, hoisted the flag.

Wilson was the first president to attend a World Series game (Philadelphia, 1915) but he appears to have liked baseball even when rank amateurs were playing. In 1918 he not only threw out the first ball for the annual congressional game, but sat through to the last out of a Republican rout of the Democrats with a score of 19-5.

Yet major-league baseball suffered during Wilson's presidency because of the military draft in World War I. Theatrical performers — actors, singers, magicians — were exempted because, the government reasoned, they provided essential recreation. Ballplayers got no such favor, and on May 23, 1918, General Enoch Crowder, provost marshal of the Army and the man in charge of conscription, issued an order that headline writers called "work or fight." By July 1, Crowder said, young men should get into essential work or face induction into the armed forces.

Presidents Ban Johnson of the American League and John K. Tener of the National League reacted with strong, contradictory statements. One day Johnson said he would like to "close every theater, ball park, and place of recreation in the country and make people realize that they were in the most terrible war in the history of the world." A month later he said baseball should be exempted as essential.

Tener, a former governor of Pennsylvania, foresaw national disaster if baseball were curtailed. The game, he said, was a "moral and spiritual production. ... Simply because what baseball produces is intangible I do not think it can be called non-essential or not productive."

But it was, and players were leaving their teams to return to the farm or take work in war factories, many of which hired them to play on company baseball teams. Eddie Ainsmith, 26, a catcher for the Washington Senators, appealed the loss of his draft exemption that resulted from the "work or fight" edict. Ainsmith was the epitome of the baseball journeyman — a career .232 hitter with no power — but his was the test case for baseball's claim that it was essential.

On July 19, Secretary of War Newton Baker announced that baseball was not essential and Ainsmith would be drafted unless he took an essential job. Teams feared they would lose all their players, and Ban Johnson announced that the American League season would end two days later, after games on July 21.

But the teams ignored Johnson and kept playing, although players were leaving. The remainder of the 1918 season was in question, and it appeared certain that major-league baseball would not be played in 1919 if the war continued. Tener urged Wilson to intervene. "If the order is made effective," he warned the president in a letter, "this large and respectable business will be ruined."

Tener followed up with a telegram, saying he was on his way to Washington and had to see the president. Wilson didn't reply publicly, but brushed off the excitable National League president with a note to his chief White House aide. "How am I to escape this?" the president wrote. "There is no earthly use in my discussing the baseball situation referred to by ex-Governor Tener."

In fact, however, Wilson did intervene, at least a little. On July 27 the White House made public a letter to the editor of *Spalding's Baseball Guide*. "The President asked me to acknowledge receipt of your letter of July 26th and to say that he sees no necessity at all for stopping or curtailing the baseball schedule," a Wilson aide wrote.

Baker and Crowder, who after all worked under Wilson, struck a compromise. They agreed to let the baseball season continue until the weekend of September 1, with another week or so for the World Series. That was fine with the baseball owners. Attendance was down, and cutting 30 days from the baseball schedule saved them 30 days worth of player salaries. World War I ended on November 11, 1918, sparing Wilson the distress of presiding over a summer without baseball, as 1919 would have been under continued wartime rules.

As president, Wilson never saw another major-league game, though he was a genuine baseball enthusiast. His health was shattered by the strain of peace negotiations and he suffered a stroke after a grueling, unsuccessful nationwide campaign to generate support for the League of Nations. Embittered by the rejection of his ideals and the overwhelming triumph of his enemies in the 1920 presidential election, he remained in Washington after leaving the White House, living as a semi-recluse, isolated from old friends.

But the failing ex-president found solace in baseball. A downstairs room of his Washington house was called "the dugout," and there Wilson met daily with his secretary, Randolph Bolling, to review box scores and game stories. He traveled repeatedly to Griffith Stadium to watch the Senators play, always by special arrangement with Clark Griffith. Wilson's car would enter the stadium through a special gate and park by the Washington bullpen. From there, Wilson would watch the game, with Washington players standing by to make sure no foul ball struck the ailing man's car. Al Schacht, a Senators coach and the first celebrated baseball clown, wrote in his autobiography that he often talked with Wilson. "He usually stayed right to the end of the games, and I would say he knew baseball better than the average fan," Schacht wrote.

## WHERE THERE'S SMOKE? — A 1990S WHOPPER

■ Presidential legends mostly tend to be hoary oldies, but a new 1990s doozie has cropped up to the effect that an unnamed scout saw Woodrow Wilson pitch at Princeton and reported back to his team that he "threw smoke."

Forget it. For starters, Wilson was not a pitcher and nothing published during his lifetime even hints at this possibility. The only position he played was at Davidson where he was a center fielder. Second, he did not play on the varsity at Princeton, but rather with a scruffy nine known as the Bowery Boys, recruited exclusively from the rooming house where Wilson boarded. Finally, Wilson graduated in the class of 1879, but there is no evidence that the slang use of the term "smoke" for speed appeared for many years to come. According to the linguistic record, the first time "smoke" was used in this context in print was in 1912. The assertion — along with a preposterous claim that he played semi-pro ball in Virginia — appeared in a caption that appeared in an exhibit on presidents and baseball at the Nixon Library in 1992. It also asserted that Wilson combined "brains with brawn," a remarkable claim for a sickly, dyspeptic string bean of a man whose name was never, ever linked to the word "brawn." It was repeated elsewhere, including an article in the *Los Angeles Times* of July 7, 1992.

Where did this nonsensical business come from? Probably from a tongue-in-cheek line written by Jerry Izenberg of the *Newark Star-Ledger* back in 1971, about presidents and their first pitches of the season. Because Wilson saw the Senators win all three games for which he threw the opening ball, Izenberg facetiously tagged him "Woodrow 'Big Train' Wilson" and noted that he "was no young kid out of Princeton who threw pure smoke as the scouts say ...."

# PRESIDENT, AT HIS FIRST BALL GAME IN 2 YEARS, SEES GRIFFS AND TIGES IN TIE

## President Throwing Out Ball to Start Red Cross Benefit Game

Left to right: Mrs. Wilson; President Wilson; Clark Griffith and Admiral Grayson.

**CLIPPING**

**The president at the ballpark is always a topic for news coverage. Here Woodrow Wilson, accompanied by his wife and the White House physician, tosses out the first pitch at a World War I charity game on May 24, 1918. It was to be the last game Wilson attended as president.**

Wilson by then bore little resemblance to the enthusiastic young man who played baseball with his housemates at Princeton and who avidly followed the progress of the varsity nine. Although troubled by poor health, his interest in sports was always keen. (While teaching at Wesleyan University, he earned a reputation as a football pioneer by outlining plays on a blackboard, an innovation that earned him a footnote in football history.)

Later, as professor of government at Princeton, he was a singularly loud and obnoxious presence at baseball games who was long remembered for his disagreements with umpires. He would shout and wave his umbrella at the men in blue at the hint of a bad call against Princeton. On one occasion he actually stalked onto the field to protest a decision. The game was stopped so the ranting professor could be removed. When Wilson wasn't arguing calls, he was rooting. At both Wesleyan and Princeton he was remembered as the man at the baseball game who, in the words of his cousin Mary Hoyt, "waved his umbrella and cheered ...."

In 1970, at the Woodrow Wilson House in Washington, a paper on Wilson was delivered by Sabin Robbins of the National Trust for Historic Preservation which contained this telling assessment: "High-strung, plagued by headaches and dyspepsia all his life, Wilson valved off tensions at sports events."

**HAPPY DAY**
**President and Mrs. Wilson, to his right, enjoy Opening Day 1916.**

# WOODROW WILSON:
# SPORTS MASTERMIND

■ Many presidents were better students than athletes as young men and turned their bookish talents to managing and coaching sports teams. None was more successful and innovative than Woodrow Wilson.

As a student at Princeton he was an active manager-coach for the football team and devised a hard-to-grasp waxed-canvas shirt — the ancestor of the breakaway jersey — that was worn by the undefeated Tiger eleven of 1878. He boosted gate prices and was the first ever to use football income to finance other sports — in this case baseball.

His most remarkable innovation was introduced when he was a young professor at Wesleyan University in Middletown, Connecticut. In pregame meetings with the football team, he outlined plays on a blackboard, making him the father of the chalk talk. This secret weapon allowed a series of five or six plays to be run without a signal. When lowly Wesleyan upset the University of Pennsylvania at the end of the 1889 season, a large group of rejoicing students paraded to Wilson's house to serenade him. Thus the spindly intellectual managed to earn the accolade "one of the founders of modern football."

But at the end of his life, baseball provided a calming refuge. He died in Washington on February 3, 1924. One more summer and he would have seen the Washington Senators win their first pennant.

## 1918 OPENER

Newly inaugurated president Woodrow Wilson takes the ball from Clark Griffith, the man who persuaded the president to throw out the first pitch.

# CHAPTER V

# The Good Scout

*Warren Harding owned a piece of a minor-league team and sent two stars to the majors.*

**W**arren Gamaliel Harding may not have been much of a president, but he played ball with a future major-leaguer, twice owned part of his hometown's threadbare minor-league team, and prided himself on the discovery of two big-league stars.

He also hosted Babe Ruth at the White House, saw the first shutout at Yankee Stadium, and kept an expert scorecard.

Nominated by the Republican Party in the "smoke-filled room" convention of 1920, Harding campaigned for the presidency from the front porch of his home in Marion, Ohio. Day after day

**WAR HERO**
**President Harding at the 1922 Washington opener with future President Herbert Hoover (far left, arms folded), Mrs. Florence K. Harding (to Harding's right) and (in uniform, facing Harding) General John J. Pershing, hero of World War I.**

## TWO PRESIDENTS
**Two real fans, as well: President Harding and his secretary of commerce, Herbert Hoover (seated, to Harding's right), who became president in 1929.**

**LAP LANDER**

**Walter Johnson's son, Walter Jr., was playing in front of the dugout at the 1922 opener on April 12. Harding called him over and took the boy in his lap, where he sat for the first inning. "This is a mighty fine boy you have here," he told the great pitcher.**

he greeted politicians, grandly escorted through Marion by brass bands. He nodded sagely as representatives of what we now call "interest groups" pressed their causes upon him. He got tired of it.

Then one day a Brooklyn baseball writer, Thomas S. Rice, showed up to interview him about sports. Harding wouldn't stop talking, letting politicians wait. He recalled playing first base as a boy with Bob Allen, a big-league shortstop for seven years, a manager for two seasons and by 1920 owner of the Little Rock club of the Southern Association.

Harding also owned the newspaper in Marion, and as a civic booster and baseball fan owned part of the town's baseball team, which played in the Ohio-Pennsylvania League in 1907 and the Ohio State League in 1911. He lost money, but he boasted to Rice of his success in developing big-league stars Jake Daubert and Wilbur Cooper.

He worked hard to get them promoted, finally landing Daubert a slot with the Brooklyn Dodgers in 1910. Daubert, a first baseman like Harding, twice led the National League in batting and wound up his 15-season career with a lifetime batting average of .303.

Cooper got to the Pirates in 1912, won 20 or more games four times, and finished with 216 wins in 15 seasons. These days, any veteran scout would be proud to land two prizes like Daubert and Cooper in a career.

**LET 'ER RIP**

**Harding cuts loose at the 1921 opener. Secretary of Commerce Herbert Hoover is second from left, seated. Mrs. Harding (mouth open, wearing a big hat) is to Hoover's left.**

In 1920, the year he was elected president, Harding played first base in a charity game in his hometown of Marion, Ohio. He got a hit, but a thrown ball injured his finger, and he retired from the field.

Harding liked a good time and convivial company, more than was good for him. He was well-supplied with bootleg liquor and his cronies busily enriched themselves with corrupt deals. H.L. Mencken considered him an ignoramus; Alice Roosevelt Longworth said, "Harding was not a bad man. He was just a slob."

Harding played golf and poker, and welcomed Babe Ruth to the White House several times. He had a good arm on opening days, and on April 24, 1923, he traveled to New York to see the Washington Senators play in the Yankees' new stadium. Walter Johnson, the great Washington pitcher, recalled the occasion in his memoirs. "I distinctly remember the last game President Harding witnessed," Johnson wrote. "He was in New York and showed up at Yankee Stadium unannounced. Before the game he sent for me, and as we shook hands he said, just as informally as possible: 'Well, Walter, I came out to root for Washington.'"

As things turned out, the president saw the first shutout in Yankee Stadium, pitched by Sad Sam Jones of the Yanks. Ruth homered in the Yankees' 4-0 victory. Harding died in office four months later.

## THE BABE

Harding congratulates Ruth after a Bambino home run in a New York City game on April 24, 1923. Ruth joined the president at the White House several times, but Harding rooted for the Washington Senators. Sportswriter Thomas S. Rice claimed: "He [Harding] was the sort that gloomed and did not enjoy his supper at the White House if he had seen the Washington team lose. On the contrary, he felt it was a pretty good world, and things would soon come out all right in Europe or elsewhere, if he had seen the Senators win."

# CHAPTER VI
# The Reluctant Fan

*Calvin Coolidge embraced baseball for political gain but wife Grace genuinely adored the game.*

Calvin Coolidge was the first president to play real political hardball. Coolidge didn't care for baseball, and he came across as an iceberg — "a calculating, unexcitable man who showed nothing," according to Clark Griffith, owner of the Washington Senators. Coolidge was vice president under Warren Harding, and when Harding died in August 1923 Coolidge became president.

The Republicans nominated him for president in 1924, but worried that his taciturn personality wouldn't sell. Alice Roosevelt Longworth, Teddy's daughter, said Coolidge looked "like he had been weaned on a pickle." As the election approached, the Washington Senators, of all teams, edged the Yankees for the pennant. Coolidge's handlers decided to make a fan out of Silent Cal. The idea was that a couple of hours in a box seat at the World Series would win more votes than a couple of weeks of campaign speeches. One supporter sent this telegram to Frank Stearns, a White House aide:

INDUCE PRESIDENT TO TENDER RECEPTION AND BANNER TO JOHNSON AND WASHINGTON TEAM OUR AMERICAN PRINCES FEEL IT HIGHLY DESERVED AND FURTHERMORE WOULD BE ONE OF FINEST POLITICAL STROKES IN HISTORY.

LIBRARY OF CONGRESS

**TOPS IN TOWN**

President Coolidge, prior to a game on June 18, 1925, presents Senators star Walter Johnson with plaque commemorating Johnson's selection as the 1924 American League MVP. Coolidge admired the soft-spoken Johnson, perhaps the greatest pitcher of all time. On August 2, 1927, Coolidge made political headlines by declaring "I do not choose to run for president in 1928." When his audience strained for an explanation, Coolidge instead veered to the subject of Walter Johnson's character: "I do not suppose all the youth of America would care to be big league ballplayers, but I know they all would profit if the character of Walter Johnson was emulated by them."

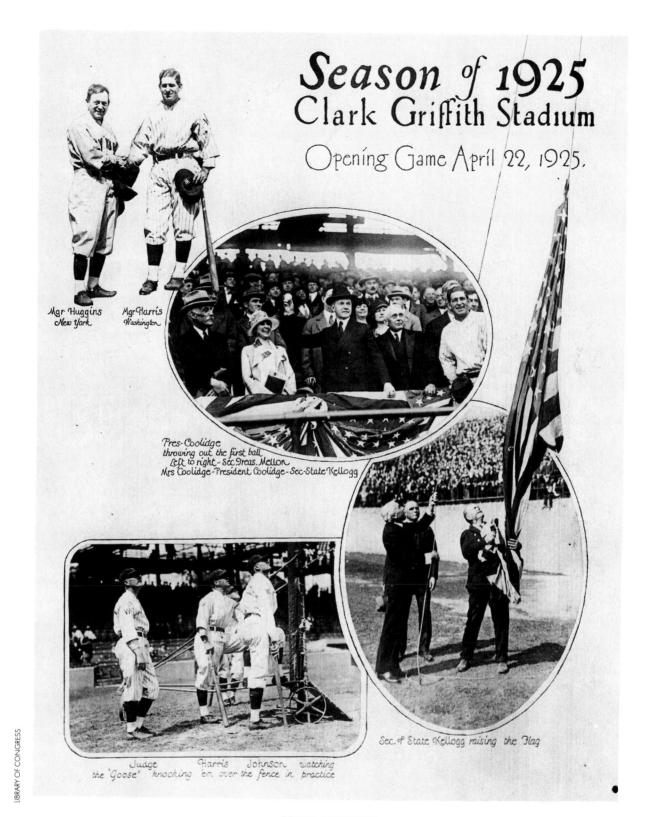

**Season of 1925**
**Clark Griffith Stadium**
Opening Game April 22, 1925.

Mgr Huggins
New York

Mgr Harris
Washington

Pres-Coolidge
throwing out the first ball
Left to right - Sec.Treas. Mellon
Mrs Coolidge-President Coolidge-Sec-State Kellogg

Sec. of State Kellogg raising the Flag

Judge    Harris    Johnson    watching
the 'Goose' knocking 'em over the fence in practice

### 1925 OPENER
***Upper left*** in this montage from a baseball program are opposing managers Miller Huggins of the Yankees and Bucky Harris of the Senators. *Center*, President Coolidge throwing out the first ball. From left to right are Treasury Secretary Andrew Mellon, Grace Coolidge, Secretary of State Frank Kellogg and Bucky Harris. *Lower right*, Kellogg raises the flag. *Lower left*, Senators Joe Judge, Harris and Walter Johnson watch slugger Goose Goslin take batting practice. The Senators mauled the Yanks 10-1.

**AVENUE OF SENATORS**
Some 100,000 people line Pennsylvania Avenue on October 1, 1924, to watch the Washington Senators parade to the Ellipse for a speech by President Coolidge. The Senators had just won the American League pennant.

# WALTER JOHNSON AND THE MISSING BASEBALLS

■ Walter Johnson pitched opening games before four presidents — Taft, Wilson, Harding and Coolidge. He managed Washington openers before a fifth president, Herbert Hoover. He got all five presidents to autograph the opening-pitch ball. He even arranged to get a ball autographed by Teddy Roosevelt, who never attended a Washington opener.

Johnson treasured his collection, each personally inscribed by a president, and kept the balls in a special display box.

Autographed baseballs were commonplace at the Johnson household. "Anything less than a Babe Ruth we used to hit around the yard," Johnson's son, Edwin, recalled in a 1968 interview. But no one was allowed to touch the presidential baseballs. Realizing their significance, Edwin donated them in 1968 to the Baseball Hall of Fame and Museum in Cooperstown, New York, where they were the centerpiece of a "Presidents' Room" display, still in their case.

In 1978 Johnson's grandson, Hank Thomas of Washington, traveled to Cooperstown to begin research for a biography of his famous grandfather. The case was on display, with only a picture of the balls. Thomas asked to see them. Three days later Thomas asked again. He was ushered into an office and told the balls had been stolen five years before. Hall of Fame officials had kept the theft secret for fear that publicity would lead to further thefts.

The presidential baseballs have never turned up. Their value is incalculable, but several experts agree that the balls would be worth as much as half a million dollars. One of the missing balls is the very first opening ball tossed by Taft in 1910.

The Senators clinched the pennant in Boston on September 29th and returned in triumph to Washington on October 1. Thousands of screaming fans met their train. Thousands more lined Pennsylvania Avenue for a victory parade. Riding in shiny new convertibles, led by a police escort, the players paraded to the Ellipse, where Coolidge greeted them outdoors on a bunting-draped platform. He gave an inspiring speech, promised to attend the World Series, and suggested that Congress adjourn so members also could attend.

It was just the right tonic for the Coolidge campaign. "I believe that the speech to the Washington team has been immensely valuable as showing an entirely new side of his character," enthused Coolidge's aide, Edward T. Clark.

For the World Series, Coolidge had just the right coach — his wife. Grace Coolidge was an avid baseball fan who sometimes went to games without her husband, and on opening days stayed in the presidential box after Coolidge slipped out early. She kept a perfect scorecard. "Where did you learn that?" Clark Griffith asked her one day. "At college," she replied. "I was the official scorer for our baseball team."

It was Washington's first pennant. The White House was deluged with ticket requests from loyal Republicans, and obliged them by the dozen until the Senators said they could spare no more. On October 4, with appropriate dignity, Coolidge took his place in the presidential box and became the first president to attend a World Series opener. It lasted 12 innings, the New York Giants winning 4-3. The president not only stayed; he smoked a cigar. It played well in Peoria, where an advertising man named Harry Clatfelter wrote this to Coolidge:

"Thank God for a president who is human enough to chuck the whole United States inside his roll top and slam the lid down while he goes out to see his home town team play a World's Series baseball game."

**WHITE HOUSE VISITORS**
**Calvin Coolidge chats with the Washington Senators outside the White House. That's Walter Johnson demonstrating his pitching grip to Coolidge while manager Bucky Harris stands to Coolidge's right and Clark Griffith, owner of the team, is to Johnson's left. The Senators were fresh from Boston, where they clinched the 1924 American League pennant.**

The second game was played on Sunday. Coolidge stayed home in deference to voters who disapproved of frivolous activities on the Sabbath. Someone started a rumor that the president was at the ballpark, and White House aides assured worried Republicans that it wasn't so. Coolidge did not attend, one aide wrote to a gentleman in Pittsburgh, adding this: "P.S. I did."

The series moved to New York, then back to Washington with the Giants up three games to two. Again the Coolidges were there, and the Senators squared the series at three games each.

Game seven provided one of the most exciting World Series finishes in history. Walter Johnson, 36 years old but pitching in his first series, had lost two games, distressing many fans. With the seventh game tied 3-3 after eight innings, Johnson took over in relief for the Senators.

## TO THE ARMORED KNIGHTS OF THE BAT AND BALL

■ "They are a great band, these armored knights of the bat and ball. They are held up to a high standard of honor on the field, which they have seldom betrayed. While baseball remains our national game our national tastes will be on a higher level and our national ideals on a finer foundation. By bringing the baseball pennant to Washington you have made the National Capital more truly the center of worthy and honorable national aspirations."

— President Calvin Coolidge, addressing the Washington Senators outside the White House on October 1, 1924, after the Senators clinched their first American League pennant.

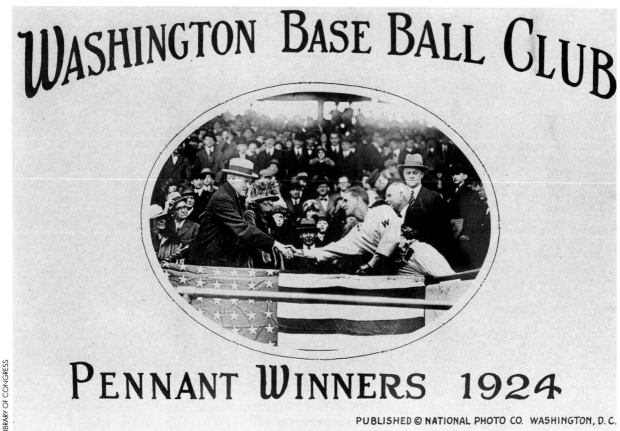

WASHINGTON BASE BALL CLUB

PENNANT WINNERS 1924

PUBLISHED © NATIONAL PHOTO CO. WASHINGTON, D.C.

**CHAMPIONS**
**President Coolidge congratulates Bucky Harris, young player-manager of the Washington Senators.**
**Harris invited the Coolidges to his wedding on October 1, 1926, and they proudly attended.**

Again and again the Giants threatened but did not score. One *Washington Post* writer had his eye on the presidential box.

"Time and again as tense moments tumbled after each other in the thrilling battle President Coolidge fell into the spirit which held the throng, sitting rigidly on the edge of his seat waiting for the next play which might decide the game," he wrote. "He was the first to his feet as the crowd rose en masse to cheer Walter Johnson entering the box in the ninth. He pounded his hands heartily as Walter returned four times from the box with the Giants still at his mercy."

In the home 12th, with Muddy Ruel on second base, Earl McNeely hit a routine ground ball to third. It hit a pebble and bounded over the head of third baseman Fred Lindstrom. Ruel scored, and the Senators were world champions.

## RUTHIAN CANDOR

■ Before a game in Washington, players of the visiting New York Yankees lined up to meet President Coolidge, who slowly walked down the line exchanging polite greetings. He came to Babe Ruth.

Coolidge: "Mr. Ruth."

Ruth, wiping his forehead with a handkerchief: "Hot as hell, ain't it, Prez?"

## GOOD POLITICS

**President Coolidge reads a congratulatory speech to the American League champion Washington Senators, October 1, 1924, while Senators manager Bucky Harris holds a trophy presented by the president. Walter Johnson is behind Coolidge, next to an unidentified child. The others, like Coolidge, are members of the Cabinet and government officials basking in the team's popularity.**

Fans grabbed Johnson and brought him to Coolidge, who shook his hand. "Nice work," the president said blandly. "I am glad you won." His reputation for taciturnity was intact, but Grace Coolidge was undone. "Nor did she just cheer," reported *The Sporting News*. "She jumped up and down on both feet, waved her arms, yelled, called out to Walter Johnson .... The picture of sedateness on her arrival, she left as rumpled, as tired, and as happy as the thousands of other fans."

Coolidge quickly came up with a sound bite. "The three contests which I have witnessed maintained throughout a high degree of skill and every evidence of a high class sportsmanship that will bring to every observer an increased respect for and confidence in our national game," he said.

It was just three weeks before the election. *The Sporting News*, the "Bible of baseball," sang Coolidge's praises as "a great and sincere friend" of the game, and said that his presence showed "no New England man ever was born who does not know baseball."

The Democratic candidate, John W. Davis, didn't have a chance. Coolidge won in a landslide. But by Opening Day of 1925 the president had lost his touch. When the seventh inning rolled around, the nation's foremost fan for the Washington Senators stood up and stretched for the visiting New York Yankees. Whoops! Mrs. Coolidge grabbed his coattail and pulled him down.

## NATIVE AMERICAN
In the documentary "Fifty Years Before Your Eyes,"
President Coolidge's wearing of an Indian headdress
at a ball game was preserved for all time.

# CHAPTER VII

# The Shortstop

*Herbert Hoover loved baseball, but Babe Ruth endorsed his opponent and fans booed him at the World Series.*

N o president loved baseball more than Herbert Hoover, but he didn't really want to go to Philadelphia for the third game of the 1931 World Series on October 5. The Great Depression had reached panic proportions. Over 2200 banks had failed in 1931 alone, stripping families of their savings, since back then deposits were not insured. Unemployment was continuing to rise (it would peak at 25% in 1933).

Hoover as a matter of principle considered relief programs a local responsibility, and continued to express optimism that recovery was just around the corner. Members of his Cabinet, notably Treasury Secretary Andrew Mellon, held to the belief that the 1929 stock market crash was a

HOOVER PRESIDENTIAL LIBRARY

### PRESIDENTIAL AUTOGRAPHING
**President Hoover signs a ball for Gabby Street, manager of the St. Louis Cardinals, before the third game of the 1931 World Series at Philadelphia's Shibe Park, where he was booed by fans.**

## SALAD DAYS

**Secretary of Commerce Hoover opens the sandlot baseball season in Washington, D.C., sometime between 1921 and 1928. Although he played shortstop as a youth, Hoover's opening pitches tended to be wild.**

## TED WILLIAMS AND HERBERT HOOVER

■ The Depression may have marred Herbert Hoover's reputation, but he had a lifelong fan in Ted Williams, the great slugger. When Williams was managing the Washington Senators from 1969 through 1971, he told Shelby Whitfield, the Senators' play-by-play broadcaster, who he considered America's greatest president ever — and perhaps the world's greatest leader.

"Not Lincoln, Washington, Alexander Graham Bell, Julius Caesar, Napoleon, Attila the Hun," Williams said. "Not Jefferson, Wilson, Churchill, not even FDR, but Herbert, by God, Hoover. Every cure of the Depression was thought up by Hoover. Here is a man who is blamed for things that were not his fault, yet he never complained, and continued to help his country for the rest of his life. To me, that's a real man."

Williams, a student of hitting, also would have liked Hoover's philosophy of baseball, because the president preferred high-scoring games. Hoover suggested that batters get four strikes instead of three. "I want more runs in baseball itself," he said in a speech to baseball writers after his presidency. "When you were raised on a sandlot, where the scores ran 23 to 61, you yearn for something more than a 5 to 2 score. You know as well as I do that the excitement, temperature and decibels of any big game today rise instantly when there is someone on base. It reaches ecstasy when somebody makes a run."

He said good pitching bored him. "I protest that we fans are being emotionally starved and frustrated by long periods of perfect performance of these batteries," he said. "Moreover, when there are nothing but strikes and balls going on, you relapse into your worries over the Bank of England, or something else."

temporary correction and the government should allow economic forces to run their course. "Liquidate labor," Mellon advised, "liquidate stock, liquidate the farmers."

The Democrats were on the attack at this inaction, and had scored gains in the 1930 midterm elections. Hoover, a sober and able man with years of sterling government service, was now a president besieged, his name part of the vocabulary of the Depression: shantytowns of the homeless were known as "Hoovervilles," pockets turned inside-out were "Hoover flags" and newspapers were "Hoover blankets."

On October 4, 1931, Hoover met past midnight with leaders of the banking and insurance industries, trying to persuade them to unite in a plan that might rescue the banking and credit industries.

"They constantly reverted to a proposal that the government do it," Hoover wrote in his memoirs. "I returned to the White House after midnight more depressed than ever before. I had long since arranged to attend the World Series at Philadelphia the next day. Although I like baseball, I kept this engagement only because I felt that my presence at a sporting event might be a gesture of reassurance to a country suffering from a severe attack of 'jitters'."

Newspapers had previewed Hoover's appearance, so fans quickly recognized the president and his wife as they came onto the field from a private entrance and took seats in a box. The starting pitchers, Lefty Grove of the Philadelphia Athletics and Burleigh Grimes of the St. Louis Cardinals, stopped warming up in deference to the president. Mrs. Hoover looked smart in a burgundy outfit and an orchid corsage. Hoover waved his gray hat and smiled.

Light applause swept the stands. Then a few boos. More boos. The booing became almost a roar, and evolved into a chant. Economics might have been on Hoover's mind, but the fans made their feelings known: "We want beer! We want beer! We want beer!" National Prohibition was in its 12th year, and bitterly controversial. Hoover supported it, but a Hoover-appointed commission had concluded that enforcement was a failure. Of the fans' chant, Joe Williams of the New York *World-Telegram* and *Sun* wrote, "it has the swing and resonance of a college cheer at a football game. It is a shocking manifestation of bad manners and lack of respect .... This must be the first time a president ever has been booed in public, and at a ball game, of all places."

With the Cardinals leading 4-0 after eight innings, the loud-speaker system — only a year old, and one of the first in the major leagues — brought word that the president and Mrs. Hoover were leaving. "Silence. Silence, please," the announcer said. He asked the fans to remain seated.

The Hoovers walked onto the field, past the Athletics' dugout, toward the special exit. The fans booed loudly and renewed their chant. "We want beer! We want beer!"

Joe Williams, the sports columnist, was distressed. "We can only imagine how Mr. Hoover, a real sportsman, who had taken a day off to relax at a ball game, a privilege at the command of even the most obscure citizen, must have felt as the train sped him back to his awesome duties in a troubled and distressed Washington," he wrote.

In his memoirs, Hoover indicated it was even worse than that. "I was not able to work up much enthusiasm over the ball game, and in the midst of it I was handed a note informing me of the sudden death of Senator Dwight Morrow," he wrote. "He had proved a great pillar of strength in the Senate and his death was a great loss to the country and to me. I left the ball park with the chant of the crowd ringing in my ears: 'We want beer!'"

*"You amaze me, Yog. You've now become such a world figure that you drew more applause yesterday than either Prime Minister Nehru or Herbert Hoover. Can you explain it?"*

*"Certainly. I'm a better hitter."*

— Exchange between Joe Garagiola and Yogi Berra after Nehru, the prime minister of India, and former President Hoover were introduced to the crowd at Yankee Stadium before a 1960 World Series game.

## HALL OF FAMERS
Three days after his 86th birthday, Hoover threw out the first ball for an Old-Timers' game at Yankee Stadium on August 13, 1960. All three former players in the picture were members of the Baseball Hall of Fame — left to right: Red Ruffing, Bob Feller and Joe DiMaggio.

## LIKE OLD TIMES

Former president Hoover in 1940 swaps stories with (left to right) Honus Wagner, legendary shortstop of the Pittsburgh Pirates; William Benswanger, president of the Pirates; and Babe Ruth. The occasion was a Baseball Writers' Association of America fundraiser for the Finnish Relief Fund.

## ROD AND REEL

President Hoover enjoyed fishing as well as baseball, and established a rustic presidential retreat, "Camp Hoover," in the Blue Ridge mountains of Virginia near what is now Shenandoah National Park. Hoover always wore a coat and tie while fishing, at least when photographers were present.

Franklin Roosevelt chose a site in Maryland's Catoctin Mountains as his getaway and called it "Shangri-La." When Dwight Eisenhower became president he changed the site's name to "Camp David" after grandson and future baseball buff David Eisenhower.

63

A Philadelphian named William Macdonald wrote Hoover the next day that "it was an error for you to attend the ball game here .... I am sorry to say this, for the people love your genial presence, and honor your real greatness, but the fact remains that while you were at the ball game this city was in the midst of a veritable financial panic and banks with deposits of approximately $25,000,000 closed their doors."

It wasn't the first time Hoover had disappointed a World Series fan. On October 14, the president had attended the fifth and final

HOOVER PRESIDENTIAL LIBRARY

### RICKEY AND HOOVER
**Hoover in 1943 with newscaster Lowell Thomas (left) and Branch Rickey, general manager of the Brooklyn Dodgers. Late in life Hoover and his wife lived at the Waldorf Astoria Hotel in New York. Hoover liked the American League Yankees but rooted hardest for the Dodgers, and attended many World Series games at Yankee Stadium and Ebbets Field. "Our spirits go up and down with the Dodgers' wins and losses," he told Dodgers owner Walter O'Malley, after watching the Yanks edge the Dodgers in a 1952 World Series game.**

## BEFORE THEIR TIME

A game of their own? President Hoover with members of the Hollywood Stars Girls Professional Baseball Team at the White House, September 1931. That's more than a decade before Philip K. Wrigley established the All-American Girls Professional Baseball League during World War II.

## NEW BATTERY

Jay N. "Ding" Darling, popular editorial cartoonist for *The Des Moines Register*, caricatured the 1928 Republican ticket of Herbert Hoover and Senator Charles Curtis. "Introducing the new battery" was Darling's caption; he was a close friend of Hoover's and a frequent White House visitor.

**CABINET OCCASION**
**President Hoover throws out the first ball of the 1929 season in Washington. He's surrounded by his entire Cabinet — a rare turnout of poohbahs. Hoover wore a genuine smile: the stock market crash was still six months in the future.**

game of the 1929 World Series, also in Philadelphia, and got this telegram from one Bud Garrett of Quanah, Texas:

> IF YOU DO ANY ROOTING ON BALL GAME TODAY PLEASE ROOT FOR THE CUBS AS I HAVE MY LAST FIVE SPOT ON THEM.

The Cubs led 2-0 after eight innings but the Athletics scored three in the ninth to win the game and the series. It was 15 days before the stock market collapse on Black Thursday.

Hoover was a real fan who played baseball as a youth, making the freshman team at Stanford in 1893. "I was for a short time on the baseball team as shortstop, where I was not so good," he later recalled. "In full belief in our prowess as a team, we challenged the San Francisco professional team to play us on campus. They good-humoredly accepted, but, when the score was something like 30 to 0 at the end of the fifth inning and getting dark, we called it off. In time, my colleagues decided I would make a better manager than shortstop." Hoover promoted Stanford baseball and football games, serving as a student in jobs that now would be titled business manager.

As president, Hoover strongly supported boys' baseball leagues. He threw out the first ball at an American Legion championship game and signed dozens of baseballs for use as awards to young

66

**BOOO!**
**President Herbert Hoover prepares to throw out the first ball of the third game of the 1931 World Series in Philadelphia on October 5. Fans booed the president when he arrived and again when he left, expressing their displeasure with Prohibition, which Hoover supported, by chanting "We want beer!"**

players. Like presidents today, he was not above sending congratulatory messages to baseball figures. When John J. McGraw began his 30th year as manager of the New York Giants in 1932, Hoover sent McGraw this telegram:

> I SEND YOU MY HEARTY CONGRATULATIONS UPON BEGINNING THE THIRTIETH YEAR OF YOUR GREAT CAREER AS MANAGER OF THE NEW YORK GIANTS, IN WHICH YOU HAVE DONE SO MUCH TO UPHOLD THE TRADITIONS OF CLEAN SPORTSMANSHIP IN THE MOST BELOVED NATIONAL GAME.

It was a flattering message. McGraw was often called a great manager, but "clean sportsmanship" was not his style. He replied with thanks. "It seems to me that it is a great tribute to baseball when a man as busy as the President of the United States can find time not only to send the gracious message which you sent but also that you were able to remember the years of service I put in with my present club," McGraw wrote.

He resigned a third of the way into the 1932 season and died two years later at age 60. Hoover lived to be 90, and threw out the first ball of an old-timers' game at Yankee Stadium in 1960, three days after his 86th birthday. His guests at the game included Mrs. John J. McGraw.

# SORRY, PREZ

During Herbert Hoover's 1928 presidential campaign against Democrat Al Smith a newspaper reported that Babe Ruth favored Hoover. Ruth denied it and said he was for Smith. He even posed for this campaign photo.

When Hoover appeared at Yankee Stadium a few days later, a publicity man asked Ruth to pose with the Republican nominee. "No sir," said Ruth. "Nothing doing on politics. Tell him I'll be glad to talk to him if he wants to meet me under the stands." However casually intended, it was a putdown from "The Babe," then America's most eminent celebrity. As Ruth biographer Robert W. Creamer put it, "No doubt here as to which was king."

Reporters loved it. "RUTH REFUSES TO POSE WITH HOOVER," blared the headlines. Republican newspapers threatened to cancel Ruth's syndicated column. The Babe's agent and ghost writer, Christy Walsh, quickly issued a conciliatory statement under Ruth's name, and Ruth and Hoover had their picture taken together.

Smith was governor of New York, and his presidential campaign somehow got 10 Yankees, including Ruth and the batboy, to pose for the photo seen on the following pages. Left to right, Benny Bengough,

NATIONAL BASEBALL LIBRARY

Waite Hoyt, Lou Gehrig, Tony Lazzeri, Joe Dugan, Mark Koenig, Bob Meusel, Earle Combs, Ruth and the batboy. No subs here; that's the starting lineup that won the 1928 world championship, plus pitching ace Hoyt, who won 23 games. Herbert Hoover somehow survived all this and won the election.

Although Ruth called himself a Democrat, the Republicans sought his help in 1920 after Ty Cobb endorsed Democratic presidential candidate James M. Cox. Fred Lieb, a baseball writer and friend of Ruth's, brought him word that the GOP wanted The Babe to endorse Warren Harding. "Hell, no, I'm a Democrat," Ruth replied. Then, "How much are they offering?"

The offer was $4,000 for Ruth if he would join Harding at his home in Marion, Ohio, where Harding was conducting his "front-porch" campaign. Lieb would get $1,000 for delivering Ruth to Harding's porch. Ruth bit, but was unable to find a day that fit his schedule and Harding's. Harding, too, won without The Babe's public support. Ruth's biographers say that, despite his presidential politicking, he didn't vote in a presidential election until 1944, four years before he died.

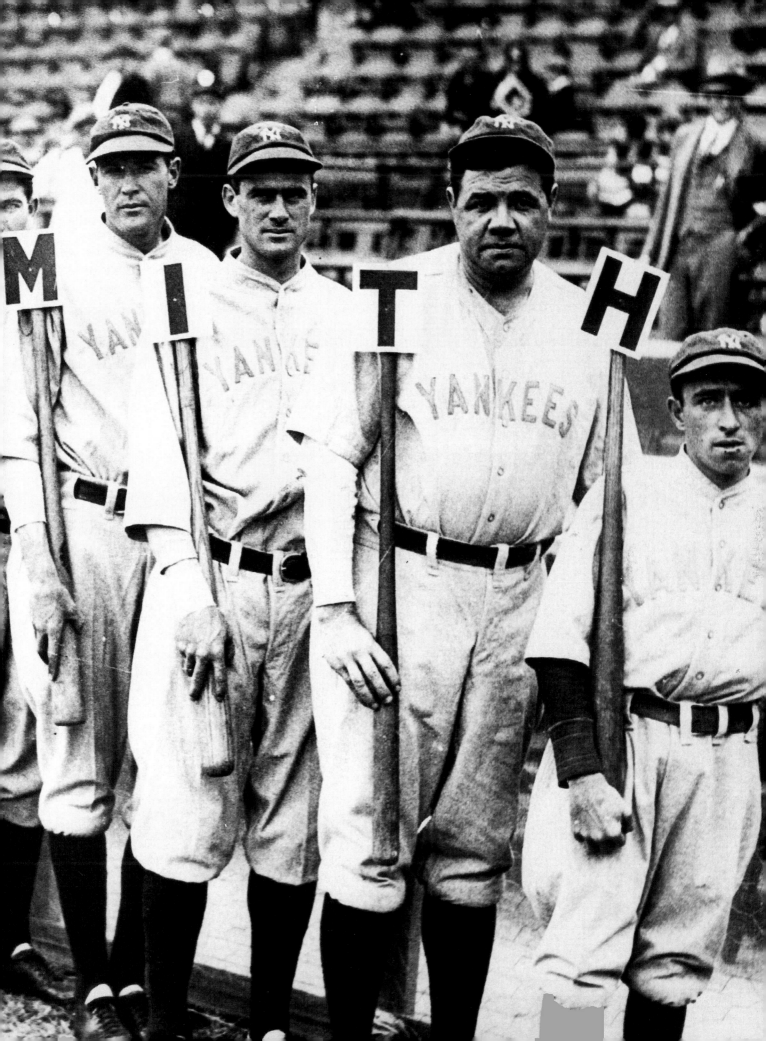

# CHAPTER VIII

# The Man Who Gave Baseball the Green Light

*Franklin Roosevelt kept major-league play alive during World War II.*

**F**ranklin D. Roosevelt was an ardent fan who seemed to relish the fuss of Opening Day, as well as the simple business of going to a ball game. "Roosevelt enjoys himself at a ball game as much as a kid on Christmas morning," wrote Harold C. Burr in the June 1939 *Baseball* magazine, adding, "Once in his field box the present president believes again that there is a Santa Claus. He gets right into the spirit of the game, munches peanuts, applauds good plays and chuckles over bad ones."

FDR let it be known that in fact he was happiest at slugfests: "I'm the kind of fan who wants to get plenty of action for my money. I get the biggest kick out of the biggest score — a game in which the hitters pole the ball into the far corners of the field, the outfielders scramble and men run the bases." He loved to bet on games with aides and Cabinet members, and was known to call Clark Griffith for pregame advice. "Griff, tell me about these pitchers," he would ask.

NATIONAL BASEBALL LIBRARY

**BOY IN THE BOATER**
The Groton baseball team of 1900, with young Franklin as manager. He had earlier given up hope of playing for the prep school team as, according to his diary, "I do not play well." At Groton he did become part of a rag-tag team known as the "Bum Base Ball Boys," which he described as a team that has "no captain but is a republic & is made up of about the worst players in the school."

71

## FLAG-RAISER

The trim, athletic man in glasses is Franklin D. Roosevelt, assistant secretary of the Navy, helping manager Clark Griffith of the Senators raise the flag to open the 1917 baseball season at Washington's American League Park. President Woodrow Wilson, an avid fan, missed that game; the nation had just entered World War I.

**1944 SUB**

**Vice President Henry Wallace tosses out the first ball in his role as relief pitcher for Franklin D. Roosevelt. In the front row, left to right, are the English archbishop of York and Senator Tom Connally. Wallace is posed with the ball and to his left are Nats manager Ossie Bluege and the ever-present Clark Griffith. Between the archbishop and Connally in the second row is Senator Harry Truman, who in three months would beat out Wallace as FDR's running mate and who in a year would become president.**

## THE MAN WHO DID THINGS DIFFERENTLY

■ Henry Wallace, vice president from 1941 until 1945, was a corn-fed American original who marched to the beat of a different drummer — and not only politically. He tossed out the first ball twice as a stand-in for President Roosevelt.

In 1942, Wallace stunned the crowd by flinging the ceremonial ball over the players' heads, all the way out to the neighborhood of second base, about 200 feet from his seat.

In 1944, the first ball was tossed by Wallace to Senators pitcher Alex Carrasquel, who was standing alone, away from the rest of the players. Had Wallace gone two for two in the erratic ball department, or was something else going on? It was later revealed that a delegation of Venezuelans, including Carrasquel, had come to Wallace to plot the first pitch. Wallace later explained that it was all in the interest of the "Good Neighbor" policy toward Latin America.

**THE HAPPY FAN**

**Franklin D. Roosevelt was an ardent fan who relished the excitement and fun of Opening Day. This is how he stood poised for the throw on Opening Day, April 17, 1935.**

## THE BIGGER THE BETTER

**Franklin Roosevelt loved action-packed games ("I get the biggest kick out of the biggest score") but his pleasure was limited by his infirmity. He was embarrassed to have the fans see his paralyzed legs and once told Clark Griffith, "If I didn't have to hobble up those steps in front of all those people, I'd be out at the park every day."**

# BASEBALL GOES TO WAR (IN WORDS)

■ It was a time for testimonials. Clark Griffith and others made sure baseball was endorsed to the hilt during the war, and that the endorsements ended up on the president's desk. Here are just a few of the collected pearls:

"You must consider that the one great tie with home for men in Africa, Australia, the Pacific or Europe, aside from family letters, is baseball scores."

— Mayor F.H. LaGuardia, New York

"If the American way of life is to survive, let baseball survive. And too, if the game should perish, then in my opinion, the larger part of what we are fighting to protect will end."

— Wendell Willkie, Republican candidate for president, 1940

NATIONAL BASEBALL LIBRARY

## A THIRD TERM

**On Opening Day 1940, Roosevelt poses with Joe Cronin (in the Boston uniform) and Bucky Harris (to Cronin's left). The Red Sox beat the Senators 1 to 0. Cronin, a stalwart of the Senators, went on to star in Boston, manage the Red Sox to a pennant, become the team's general manager and step up to the presidency of the American League.**

**Roosevelt threw out more balls than any other president; this was the next-to-last time he would participate. Once World War II began he attended no more major-league games. War clouds were already gathering when this picture was taken, and because of them Roosevelt would win election to an unprecedented third term in 1940.**

For the first eight years of his presidency, he tossed the first ball at Griffith Stadium with an unorthodox, overhanded lob. In 1940, *Washington Post* photographer Irving Schlossenberg called out, "One more, Mr. President, one more." The president obliged — and his wild throw smashed Schlossenberg's lens.

At the age of 39 Roosevelt had contracted polio and lost his ability to walk. A special ramp was erected at Griffith Stadium so he could reach his box. Alluding to this and the elaborate security arrangements which had to be made by an increasingly edgy Secret Service, Roosevelt said to Clark Griffith, "I'd come out more often, Clark, but I'm such a nuisance."

Although a friend of baseball, Roosevelt bore no good will toward baseball Commissioner Kenesaw Mountain Landis, a severe conservative. Landis loathed Roosevelt's liberal politics. He did not know the president and didn't want to. What's more, he forbade lobbying by anyone else in baseball. Ironically, Roosevelt and Landis made history with an exchange of letters in January 1942 that appeared to indicate an easy relationship between the two men. Roosevelt's letter, replying

## STANDING TALL

**Roosevelt with Joe Cronin, the Senators' player-manager, to his left at the 1933 World Series. (Clark Griffith is partially visible to Cronin's left.) In 1933, the Senators won the pennant, besting the Yankees and A's with a team carefully pieced together by Griffith and his young shortstop Cronin. To Griffith, Cronin was more than a star player and bright young man: he was the owner's son-in-law, having married Griffith's adopted daughter, who doubled as her father's secretary.**

# RED LIGHT LETTER

■ So much has been made of the "green light" letter that it is sometimes forgotten that not everybody in America was totally in agreement with it. In fact, there were people who wrote to the White House and told the president that they opposed the action. Here is an excerpt of a typical letter, replete with misspellings:

"... Mr. President, I have always loved our great National game, BaseBall, and have always wanted to be a Ball player, but because of my Physical Condition, it was never possible for me to participate in the game I love. Therefore, I had to do the next best thing, and that was to become a Died-in-the-wool Fan. And I thank God that I have been able to read about my Diamond Heroes, and to hear the games over the Radio.

"But when those Japenese made their sneaking attack on Pearl Harbor, to force us in this Awful War, my interest in BaseBall became less, and I was hoping they would discontinue the game for the Duration.

"Here are my reasons why I dont think they should be playing BaseBall, or anyother kind of ball during the War; Mr. President, I cant see a bunch of Ball Players going around the Country, getting big pay, having a good time; While Millions of other boys are fighting, Dying, Being made Cripples, Being made Sightless, for their Country. No, Mr. President, I cant get excited over a Ball game as long as we are at war. And I recommend that you suggest they close all Ball Parks for the Duration. ..."

to a handwritten letter from Landis, was the president's famous "green light" for baseball to continue during World War II.

In fact, the green light, like so many things in Washington, resulted from quiet, astute lobbying. The men behind the scenes were Clark Griffith, longtime owner of the Washington Senators, and Robert E. Hannegan, a crony and confidant of Roosevelt who held the positions of internal revenue commissioner and Democratic national chairman during Roosevelt's administration. Griffith had been baseball's unofficial lobbyist for years — a role he carefully kept from Landis. Hannegan hailed from St. Louis and was a close friend of Sam Breadon, owner of the Cardinals, and Don Barnes and William DeWitt, who owned the St. Louis Browns. After the war, Hannegan became part owner of the Cardinals — Stan Musial's boss, so to speak.

Thanks to Griffith and Hannegan, front pages bloomed with this friendly letter from FDR, which made baseball secure during

**GRAND ENTRY**

**The president arriving at Griffith Stadium to watch the All-Star Game, July 7, 1937. The men in white hats are Secret Service agents, who provided heavy protection whenever FDR visited the ballpark.**

World War II, although the quality of play sharply declined as players by the hundreds entered the armed forces.

The White House
Washington
January 15, 1942

My dear Judge:

Thank you for yours of January fourteenth. As you will, of course, realize the final decision about the baseball season must rest with you and the Baseball Club owners — so what I am going to say is solely a personal and not an official point of view.

I honestly feel that it would be best for the country to keep baseball going. There will be fewer people unemployed and everybody will work longer hours and harder than ever before.

And that means that they ought to have a chance for recreation and for taking their minds off their work even more than before.

Baseball provides a recreation which does not last over two hours or two hours and a half, and which can be got for very little cost. And, incidentally, I hope that night games can be extended because it gives an opportunity to the day shift to see a game occasionally.

As to the players themselves, I know you agree with me that individual players who are of active military or naval age should go, without question, into the services. Even if the actual quality of the teams is lowered by the greater use of older players, this will not dampen the popularity of the sport. Of course, if an individual has some particular aptitude in a trade or profession, he ought to serve the Government. That, however, is a matter which I know you can handle with complete justice.

Here is another way of looking at it — if 300 teams use 5,000 or 6,000 players, these players are a definite recreational asset to at least 20,000,000 of their fellow citizens — and that in my judgment is thoroughly worthwhile.

With every best wish,
Very sincerely yours,

Franklin D. Roosevelt

The proclamation inspired purple prose and overblown response. "If the shot that was fired at Lexington in 1775 was 'heard around the world' it is equally true that the 'Play Ball' of President Roosevelt in his letter to Commissioner Landis recently, was heard and applauded around the baseball universe," said *Baseball* magazine. In a note to the president, the sports editor of the *Chicago Sun* called it "the most notable contribution to baseball in our time," and *The Sporting News* deemed him to be "Player of the Year."

One fascinating aspect of the FDR letter was his suggestion that more night games be played. At this point in major-league history, each team was limited to seven home night games per year. Landis, among others, disapproved of night baseball. But night games improved attendance, and teams in smaller markets wanted more of them.

These needy franchises included the Senators and both St. Louis teams. Griffith and Hannegan enlisted the president in this crusade and more night games were forthcoming. The Senators, considered a special case in a city of wartime bureaucrats, were allowed 21 night games a season. Other teams got 14.

There were those who expected the green light to become an annual wartime ritual. A March 2, 1943, letter from Clark Griffith to Stephen Early, secretary to the president, said in part: "Steve, when you and your pal, Mr. [Marvin H.] McIntyre, get to the point where you can pass out the 'green light' for the coming season, please don't fail to make mention of the fact that weekend ball and night baseball would be in the best interests of the war workers in Washington as well as throughout the country." Griffith then went on to add, "I have a hard time convincing Commissioner Landis that everyone is supposed to stay on the job in the daytime." If baseball felt it deserved an annual green light, others felt left out. In early 1942, for instance, Roosevelt was asked to issue a similar green light statement for bowling. He did not oblige.

For baseball, though, Roosevelt kept the green light lit. Griffith took nothing for granted. As late as March 12, 1945, the Senators' owner left the president a fact sheet outlining 16 points of contribution from baseball since Pearl Harbor — for instance, "More than 4,000,000 soldiers and sailors have been admitted free to major-league parks alone."

The very next day, at a news conference, Roosevelt allowed that he was all in favor of the game, as long as it didn't use healthy men who could be better employed doing war work. As *The Sporting News* said, "This left the door open in case there was any widespread criticism of 17-year-old, overage or 4-F athletes who might look good in coveralls in war plants." It was fair to say that FDR had given the game a second green light.

**RITUAL OBSERVED**

**Franklin D. Roosevelt receiving his 1936 season pass from Clark Griffith and young Sandy McDonald. Griffith made a point of getting to Roosevelt every spring, even during the darkest days of World War II; he kept Roosevelt posted on baseball's contribution to the war effort.**

Exactly a month later, Roosevelt died. For fans, players and owners, there was a universal feeling that without Roosevelt baseball might have perished in the dark weeks following Pearl Harbor.

After 1941, Roosevelt never threw out another first ball. In 1942 and 1944, Vice President Henry Wallace went to Griffith Stadium in his stead. Wartime manpower chief Paul V. McNutt performed the ceremony in 1943.

Roosevelt died on April 12, 1945. The Senators opened their season a few days later, wearing black arm bands. The ball was tossed by House Speaker Sam Rayburn instead of the new president, Harry S Truman. Walter Johnson came in from his Maryland farm to participate in a ceremony in FDR's honor.

## CALLED SHOT

President-to-be Roosevelt throws out the first ball of the World Series game in Chicago on October 1, 1932, the game in which Babe Ruth hit his legendary "called shot" home run. To FDR's left is his son, James, and to his right is Mayor Anton Cermak of Chicago. In February 1933, Cermak was shot in an assassination attempt on Roosevelt in Miami and died three weeks later.

# CHAPTER IX
# The Ambidextrous Hurler

*Left-hander Harry Truman went to the ballpark more than any other president, and could throw out the first ball with either hand.*

**ME, THE SOUTHPAW**
**President Truman mugs for the camera at the 1952 Washington opener, holding a left-hander's glove. "In sports there is no 'wrong side of the tracks,'" Truman once told Ford Frick and Will Harridge, presidents respectively of the National and American leagues. "Sports is the only institution we have left where dollars, and pull, and social status don't count. If you've got the ability, you make the team. ..."**

*WASHINGTON STAR COLLECTION, MARTIN LUTHER KING LIBRARY*

On September 2, 1945, Japan formally surrendered, ending World War II. Six days later, President Harry Truman made his way to Griffith Stadium and brought peace to the home front by throwing out the first ball of a baseball game.

No chief executive had attended a game since President Roosevelt threw out the first ball of the season April 14, 1941, eight months before the Japanese attack on Pearl Harbor brought the United States into the war. Truman knew what he was doing. The president at the ballpark meant the dark days of crisis were past; his presence was a signal that peace had returned to the land and World War II was indeed over. Truman threw (wild-pitched, according to some eyewitnesses) two left-handed tosses and it was immediately realized that Truman, who was actually ambidextrous, was the first southpaw to toss one out of the presidential box.

Truman saw a real pennant-race game. The Washington Senators were playing the St. Louis Browns, defending champions of the American League. The Senators and Browns, traditional also-rans, were contending for first place with the Detroit Tigers. The level of talent was subpar since most able-bodied men were still in military uniform. The Senators beat the Browns 4-1 that day, but the Tigers wound up winning the pennant.

During his seven and one-half years as president, Truman attended sixteen games, all at Griffith Stadium. That's more than any other president, before or since. He threw some balls left-handed and he threw some right-handed.

Truman didn't flinch from controversy, even at the ballpark. On April 11, 1951, he stripped General Douglas MacArthur, a popular American hero, of his commands in the Far East. MacArthur was the general in charge of U.S. forces in the Korean War, and Truman ousted him for repeated public statements opposing the president's war policy.

MacArthur returned home to a hero's welcome. On April 19 he addressed a joint session of Congress and enthralled the nation with his emotional, nostalgic closing: "Old soldiers never die, they just fade away. And like the old soldier of the ballad, I now close my military career and just fade away, an old soldier who tried to do his duty as God gave him the light to see that duty. Goodbye."

The general was the darling of the people; the president who had fired him was the villain. The next day, April 20, was the season

83

## PEACE AT LAST

President Truman delivers the first left-handed presidential throw ever. It was September 8, 1945, six days after Japan surrendered. Mrs. Truman is to his right. To his left are Admiral William D. Leahy, White House Press Secretary Charlie Ross, and managers Ossie Bluege of the Washington Senators and Luke Sewell of the St. Louis Browns. Behind Sewell in the white hat is House Speaker Sam Rayburn.

## MINOR LEAGUES

At his office in the Federal Reserve Bank building in Kansas City, former President Truman, 69, wears the cap of the Kansas City Blues of the American Association. As his calendar shows, it's June 1953. Kansas City got a major-league team in 1955 when the Philadelphia Athletics moved west.

> *"May the sun
> never set on
> American
> baseball."*
>
> — President Harry S Truman

## FIRST UMP?

■ The anecdote: The president loved baseball when he was a kid back in Independence, Missouri, and tried his darndest to make the town team. But it was not to be. He wore glasses and his eyesight wasn't that good — so they made him an umpire.

Many kids of the late 40s and early 50s knew the story and its inevitable and oft-stated punch line, which underscored a central credo of baseball — that umpires could not see well enough to tell a ball from a strike.

This story was told by Clark Griffith and re-told by sportscaster Bill Stern and various sportswriters. It still shows up in print. But Truman himself never told the story. The closest he ever came to saying anything about his childhood and baseball was this: "You don't have to weigh 250 pounds to make good in baseball, and you don't have to be 6'7", either. I like that. I was a little fellow myself."

opener in Washington. Truman showed up, threw out the first ball, and got roundly booed. Truman was unfazed. "I was sorry to reach a parting of the way with the big man in Asia," he wrote to Dwight Eisenhower, "but he asked for it and I had to give it to him."

Truman made an annual party of Opening Day. A close friend, Lowell Mason of the Federal Trade Commission, organized a Capitol Hill luncheon for Truman and his buddies from the House and Senate. From the Capitol, they would drive to the ballpark. In 1948, a joint session of Congress started an hour early to allow time for the Truman party to attend, yet still get to Griffith Stadium in time for the first pitch.

Truman also forged a close friendship with Clark Griffith, owner of the Washington Senators. Both hailed from Missouri, both were exemplars of bootstrap success, and both had an open, straightforward way about them. Griffith called the president "Harry," and that was fine with the president.

Griffith contributed to Truman's 1948 presidential campaign, and predicted that Truman would win, although polls showed the Republican nominee, Thomas E. Dewey, far ahead. "Everyone is against Harry except the people," Griffith said. Truman's upset victory that November vindicated Griffith — and gave Truman four more opportunities to throw out the opening-day ball.

For his part, Truman volunteered to participate in a ceremony honoring Griffith on August 17, 1948, at the height of the campaign. The president gave a spontaneous speech praising the 78-year-old Griffith, and became the first president to attend a night game.

Griffith made much of his association with presidents. His office walls featured photos of presidents from Taft through Truman

## BATBOY'S SOUVENIR

**President Truman concentrates intently as he signs a ball for Bobbie Shellon, bat boy of the Washington Senators, on September 8, 1945.**

## FAST COMPANY

**Sluggers Roger Maris (left) and Mickey Mantle of the New York Yankees present a bat to former President Truman at Yankee Stadium. In 1961 Maris hit 61 home runs, breaking Babe Ruth's record, and Mantle hit 54. Truman enjoyed ball games, though as a boy he didn't play. Biographer David McCullough wrote: "He was afraid of the rough-and-tumble of the schoolyard and because of his glasses, felt incapable of any sport that involved a moving ball." He admired Bessie Wallace, his future wife, who played baseball with the skill of a boy.**

## MISSOURI CHAMPIONS

Truman shakes hands with managers Luke Sewell of the St. Louis Browns and Billy Southworth of the St. Louis Cardinals, champions of their respective leagues in 1944. The Browns and Cardinals played a "streetcar World Series" in St. Louis while Senator Truman was campaigning for vice president as Franklin D. Roosevelt's running mate. The Cardinals won; so did Roosevelt and Truman.

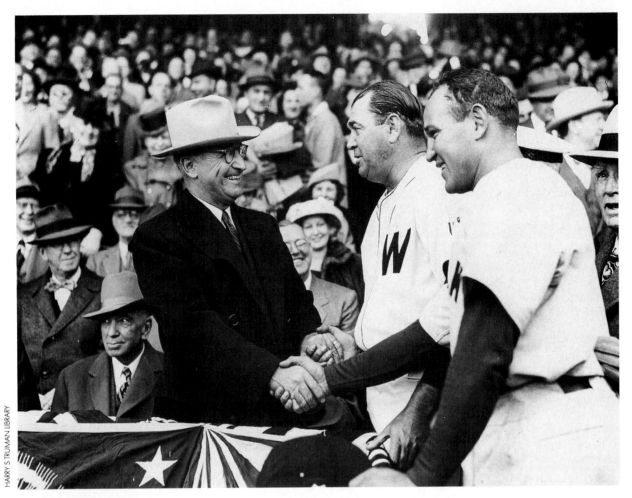

**OVERCOAT OPENER**

**President Truman greets pitchers Bobo Newsom of the Washington Senators and Allie Reynolds of the New York Yankees on Opening Day 1947. Clark Griffith, the Senators' owner and a friend of the president, is behind the pitchers.**

## THREE CHEERS FOR BESS

■ Bess Truman enjoyed hunting, fishing, skating, riding, tennis, and swimming. She played a crackerjack third base and could beat all the boys at mumblety-peg. ... One contemporary remembered Bess Truman as "the first girl I ever knew who could whistle through her teeth."
— From *WomenSports*, quoted in *Say It Again* by Dorothy Uris.

throwing out the first ball. He gave Truman a tour of the picture gallery one day, and paused at photos of President Franklin Roosevelt. He recalled that day years later, quoting himself and Truman from memory.

"Look here, Harry," Griffith said. "Look at this picture of President Roosevelt made in 1933, when he first threw out the ball, and the one made shortly before he died. Look at the difference in the two men." The first picture showed a vigorous, energetic Roosevelt in 1933. The second showed a drawn, weary FDR, accepting a 1945 season pass

89

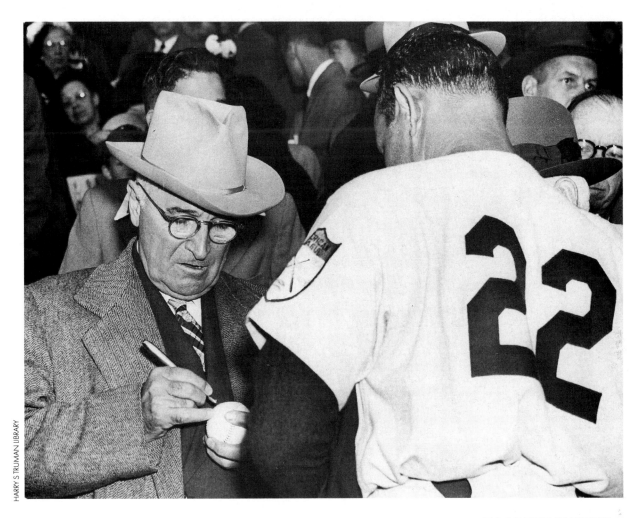

from Griffith in the annual ceremony always attended by photographers. The picture was taken in the Oval Office just a few weeks before Roosevelt's death on April 12, 1945.

"That job you got is a killing one, Harry," Griffith continued. "Don't let that happen to you."

Truman agreed. "Don't worry, Clark," he replied. "I walked into the White House and I aim to walk out of it. They will not carry me out of there in a box."

Truman returned to Independence, Missouri, after retiring from the presidency in 1953. His successor, Dwight Eisenhower, missed the 1959 opener. Vice President Richard Nixon filled in. Truman detested Nixon. That morning Griffith received this telegram from Truman:

BEST OF LUCK TO YOU ON OPENING DAY AND EVERY DAY. WATCH OUT FOR THAT NIXON. DON'T LET HIM THROW YOU A CURVE. YOUR FRIEND, HARRY TRUMAN.

**BOOS FOR HARRY**
President Truman autographing a ball at Washington's 1951 season opener on April 20. The crowd booed Truman, who had made the unpopular decision to relieve General Douglas MacArthur of his wartime command in Korea. A day earlier, MacArthur had delivered his famous farewell speech to a joint session of Congress.

**EITHER HAND**
President Truman shows off his ambidexterity before throwing out the first ball of the 1950 season at Washington. Left to right in the first row are Rear Admiral Robert Dennison, White House Naval aide; Margaret Truman, the president's daughter; Mrs. Truman; Connie Mack, long-time owner and manager of the Philadelphia Athletics; and, in profile, Vice President Alben Barkley.

# CHAPTER X

# The President Who Almost Wasn't

*Dwight Eisenhower played professional baseball under an assumed name, and might never have become president if he had been caught.*

**FORE!**

**President Eisenhower tees off at Burning Tree Club in Bethesda, Maryland. Ike loved to play golf and aroused an outcry when he decided to skip the opening game of the 1953 baseball season in Washington in favor of a golfing holiday in Augusta, Georgia. "The major leagues had counted on Ike to throw out the first ball," wrote Dan Daniel in *The Sporting News*. "They long have regarded the presence of the Chief Executive at the Griffith Stadium inaugural as a boost for the entire game, marking White House approval of our National Pastime." The opening game was rained out. Ike played golf that day, then hurried back to Washington and threw out the first ball of the rescheduled opener.**

He called it "the one secret of my life." If it had been exposed while he was at West Point, Dwight David Eisenhower might never have become the general who led the Allied Forces to victory in Europe in World War II. He might never have become president.

The genesis of the story was Eisenhower's athletic skill and his love of baseball and football. He grew up in rural Abilene, Kansas, and as a high school senior in 1909 he was president of the Abilene High School Athletic Association. On the football team, Dwight played right end while his brother, Edgar, also a senior, played fullback. On the baseball team, Dwight was the center fielder, Edgar the first baseman.

The Eisenhowers couldn't afford to send two boys to college, so Dwight and Edgar closed a deal. One would go to college while the other worked to help pay the tuition. Then they would switch roles. So Edgar went to the University of Michigan while Dwight stayed home, working in a creamery and sending most of his wages to Edgar.

In 1911, at age 21, Dwight won appointment to the U.S. Military Academy at West Point. As a freshman, he played junior varsity baseball and football. His baseball teammates included Omar Bradley, who also became a famous general of World War II. Boosted by a vigorous muscle-building program, Dwight added weight and became a star running back for the Cadets his sophomore year. *The New York Times* called him "one of the most promising backs in Eastern football."

On November 9, 1912, Army played the Carlisle Indian School, led by Jim Thorpe, who was fresh from Olympic victories in the decathlon and pentathlon. Thorpe led Carlisle to a 27-6 victory. The next week, against Tufts, a tackler brought Ike down at a clumsy angle. His knee was badly wrenched, and he injured it again shortly thereafter in a riding accident. His football days were over.

But not, apparently, his baseball days, although he never played again for Army. "Not making the baseball team at West Point was one of the greatest disappointments of my life, maybe the greatest," he later said.

As a soldier, Eisenhower rose to the top. In World War II he became the symbol of smiling, confident American leadership, the general who planned the Allied invasion of Normandy and commanded Allied forces in their sweep through Europe that finally climaxed with Germany's surrender.

In June 1945 Ike returned from Europe a national hero. A ticker tape parade was planned in New York. In a letter to General

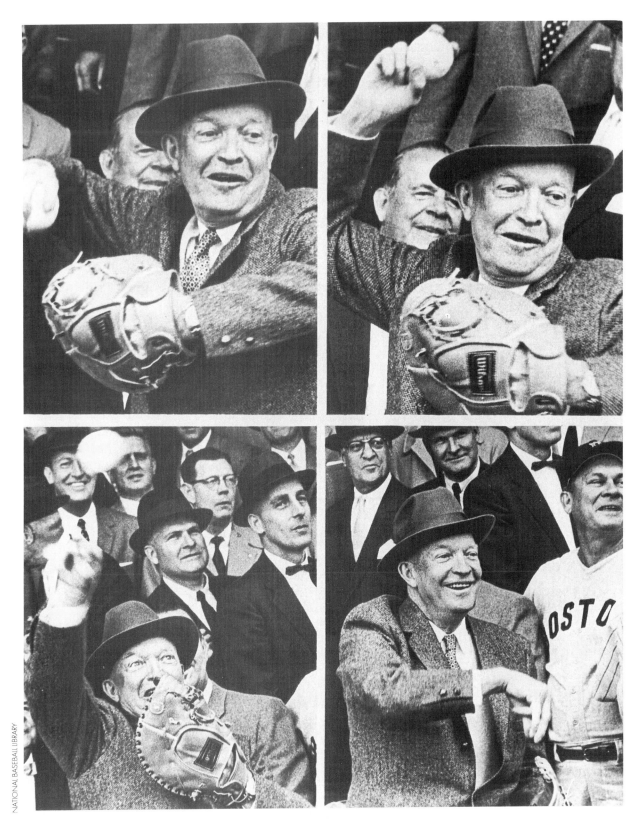

## WILSON, CF

**The opening-day throw in sequence. Note the Wilson brand name on the president's glove. Coincidentally, Wilson is the pseudonym Ike used when he played professional baseball as a youth. The Boston-uniformed man visible in the last frame is manager Pinky Higgins.**

> *"When I was a small boy in Kansas, a friend of mine and I went fishing and as we sat there in the warmth of the summer afternoon on a river bank, we talked about what we wanted to do when we grew up. I told him that I wanted to be a real major league baseball player, a genuine professional like Honus Wagner. My friend said that he'd like to be president of the United States. Neither of us got our wish."*
>
> — Dwight D. Eisenhower

George C. Marshall, Army chief of staff, Eisenhower expressed his wishes. "I have no general suggestions to make regarding the entire trip, but secretly I hope that New York has that ball game," he wrote. "I really would like to see the big leagues play again." His wish was granted, and he was paraded into the Polo Grounds to see the New York Giants play the Boston Braves on June 19, 1945. Before the game, he was introduced to the rival managers.

"Mel Ott, manager of the Giants, asked him whether it was true that he had once played semi-pro baseball," reported *The New York Times*. "The general admitted that as a youth he had done so, under the assumed name of Wilson."

In a separate story about the game, won by the Braves 9-2, the *Times* reported the same incident this way:

"Managers Ott and Coleman [Bob Coleman of the Braves] were then presented to the general. .... Then, in a brief, informal chat while hundreds of photographers were feverishly clicking their cameras from all angles, the general confided to the two skippers what he admitted to be 'the one secret of my life.'

"As a student at college, he told them, he once played professional ball under the assumed name 'Wilson.' It was in the Kansas State League, but when they asked him what position he played, he replied, 'That's my secret.'"

Back in Abilene later that month, Eisenhower reminisced to reporters about his boyhood and youth. The Associated Press carried this quote:

"I was a center fielder. I went into baseball deliberately to make money, and with no idea of making it a career. I wanted to go to college that fall, and we didn't have much money. I took any job that offered me more money, because I needed money. But I wasn't a very good center fielder, and didn't do too well at it."

After that, Eisenhower stopped talking about his brief baseball career. He surely knew that NCAA rules barred anyone who had played professionally from intercollegiate athletics. The rules against professionalism on the part of amateur athletes were stiff — so stiff that Thorpe had been stripped of his Olympic medals when it was disclosed that he played a few professional ball games. Eisenhower certainly knew about that, too. The NCAA rule:

"No student shall represent a college or university in any intercollegiate game or contest ... who has at any time received, either directly or indirectly, money, or any other consideration ... (or) who has competed for any prize against a professional."

Student athletes, Eisenhower almost surely among them, had to fill out eligibility cards with 15 questions about whether they had ever played professionally. On the bottom they had to sign this pledge: "On my honor I state that the above answers contain the whole truth, without any mental reservation."

The evidence is that Eisenhower played baseball professionally twice. Before his West Point years, he played center field one season to make money. Another summer, during his West Point years, he played a game, or a few games, in the Kansas State League under the name of Wilson. So it appears that Eisenhower skirted the NCAA rule, and probably also signed the pledge — a clear violation of the West Point honor code. Any cadet caught violating the honor code was expelled. Had Eisenhower been expelled, he would

## K MEANS STRIKEOUT

**President Eisenhower at a Washington opener, flanked by House Republican leader Joe Martin, looking at Ike's scorecard, and Calvin Griffith, owner of the Senators. Eisenhower knew his baseball and kept score. When he attended a game at the Polo Grounds in New York just after returning from the great Allied military victory in Europe, he eagerly began scoring the game — only to be interrupted by a succession of local politicians, all eager to shake the hero's hand. He soon put his scorecard aside.**

## SCHOOL DAYS

**The 1908 varsity baseball team of Abilene (Kansas) High featured two Eisenhowers — center fielder Dwight (top row, second from right) and first baseman Edgar (second row, middle). "Only by grit and perseverance," wrote the future president in the high school yearbook, did Abilene win its opener and its next four games. In describing the team's players, Ike wrote this about himself: "Makins and D. Eisenhower stick around the left and center garden patches. They work together and keep the team in good spirits by their talking."**

96

### CHUCK AND CASEY

**Ike throws a high one for managers Chuck Dressen of the Washington Senators and Casey Stengel of the New York Yankees. Eisenhower enjoyed the company of athletes. On June 5, 1953, he hosted a White House luncheon for dozens of prominent athletes including baseball stars Joe DiMaggio, Lefty Grove, Tris Speaker, Clark Griffith, Sam Rice, Joe Judge, Bill Werber, Ossie Bluege, George Case and Lu Blue. In August 1957 he invited the Little League championship team from Monterrey, Mexico, to the White House, and gave each youngster a pen.**

*Preceding pages:*

### NO, UMP!

**Ike rises to the occasion. That's Clark Griffith, the Senators owner, seated to the president's right. Jim Hagerty, the White House press secretary, is behind Eisenhower, wearing glasses and a hat.**

**"Calvin, the wife is away. How about me coming to the ball game?"**

— Call from President Eisenhower to Calvin Griffith, owner of the Washington Senators, during the 1957 season.

### BATTING CHAMP
**President Eisenhower presents Washington's Mickey Vernon with a silver bat, the trophy for winning the 1953 American League batting championship. It was Red Cross Day at Griffith Stadium, and the Senators beat the Yankees 7-3.**

never have become a general. No Crusade in Europe, no hero's welcome in New York, no "I Like Ike," no presidency.

Ike apparently knew it, because after his revelations in 1945 he stopped talking about his brief baseball career, and instructed his staff to stonewall questions on the subject. This memo, among presidential papers at the Eisenhower Library in Abilene, was written by Colonel Robert Schulz, a White House aide:

"As of August 1961, DDE indicated inquiries should not be answered concerning his participation in professional baseball — as it would necessarily become too complicated.

"The following are Mrs. Whitman's remarks to Colonel Schulz regarding the above subject:

" 'DDE did play professional baseball one season to make money, he did make one trip under an assumed name (did not say whether Wilson or not). But, he says not to answer this because it gets 'too complicated.'"

To be sure, playing a few professional ball games certainly was no sin. But under the rules of the day it could have cost Dwight David Eisenhower his place in history.

### FOUR MORE YEARS
An approving crowd looks on as Ike tosses the first ball of 1957 at the start of his second term. The managers are Chuck Dressen of the Senators and Paul Richards of the Baltimore Orioles.

E PLURIBUS UNUM

103

## WORLD SERIES

President Eisenhower throws out the first ball of the 1956 World Series at Brooklyn's Ebbets Field. That's Walter O'Malley, the Dodger president, to Ike's left, son John (in the Army uniform) and Secretary of State John Foster Dulles to his right. The Yankees' Don Larsen pitched a perfect game in the fifth game of that series, and Eisenhower wrote him a letter of congratulations. The Dodgers' pitching ace, Don Newcombe, was hammered in two starts, and Ike wrote to him, too. "I think I know how much you wanted to win a World Series game; I for one was pulling for you," he wrote. "But I suggest that when you think over this past season, you think of the twenty-seven games you won that were so important in bringing Brooklyn into the World Series." Eisenhower sent the letter to O'Malley, asking him to read it and forward it to Newcombe only if he thought it would make the pitcher feel better. "By no means would I want to remind him of something that he possibly may be trying to forget," Ike wrote.

# CHAPTER XI

# The Senators:
# The Presidents' Home Team

*"Mr. President, should the Senators leave Washington?"*

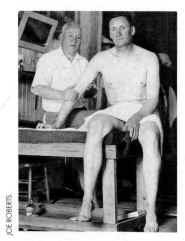

**BIG TRAIN**
**Famed pitcher Walter Johnson receives treatment after a big game.**

JOE ROBERTS

For years, presidents of the United States claimed the Washington Senators as their home team. After all, the chief executives lived in Washington, and like other residents of the nation's capital, rooted for the Senators. On Opening Day a president rode across town to the ballpark and tossed out the first ball. But try as it might, the team rarely was able to pay back fan and presidential loyalty with stellar performances. The rest of the country got a kick out of the old saw about Washington: "First in war, first in peace and last in the American League."

Aside from a few golden moments during the Walter Johnson era, the Senators' 20th-century record could be characterized as dismal. The Nats, as they were sometimes called, won only three pennants in their history, none after 1933. Not surprisingly, the poor play didn't help attendance. Nor did Griffith Stadium, what with its crumbling condition, limited parking space and deteriorating neighborhood. After topping one million in 1946, attendance steadily declined. Nowadays some teams sell more than 20,000 season tickets; the Senators sold about 50. The fans had given up on the Nats.

When Calvin Griffith took over the Senators in 1955 upon the death of his uncle and foster father, Clark Griffith, he started maneuvering to move the club out of the city to a richer location. Notwithstanding Washington's lackluster record of support, many fans were outraged at the thought of losing their woebegone team. Shirley Povich, the distinguished sports editor of *The Washington Post*, enlisted the help of his publisher, Philip Graham, in attempts to keep the Senators in Washington, where they had played since 1901.

Del Webb, co-owner of the New York Yankees, was chairman of the American League's expansion committee, and was influential among other owners. Webb owned a construction company that built military bases and other government projects. At the suggestion of Povich and Graham, a White House official passed word to Webb that President Eisenhower wanted the Senators to stay in Washington — a hint from Webb's best customer.

By 1958, however, Calvin Griffith was openly flirting with a move to Minneapolis. At a White House news conference, reporter Andrew F. Tully of the Scripps-Howard newspapers, which included the now-defunct *Washington Daily News*, put the question to President Eisenhower. Washington advocates hoped to get a strong statement from the president. Instead, they got the kind of rambling answer that Eisenhower made famous:

**FIRST TICKETS**
**After standing in line all night, Elsie Tydings gets the first tickets to Washington's first World Series, in 1924.**

Tully: "Sir, the Washington ball club is threatening or promising to leave town. (Laughter). Do you think, sir, that such a move would be justified under the circumstances?"

Eisenhower: "I would want to answer that one if. If the National, I mean if the Nationals here, the American League club here, would have a club that had a fighting chance on the average, of getting into the first division, I for one, would be down at a good number of their evening games to see them, and I would be one of their customers. Now, unfortunately, because of my present position, I am not a paying customer. (Laughter).

"And, therefore, I can't help keeping this club here. But if we could only have that, I am practically certain this city would demand that they stay here, and I think they should. But I think they should have a little bit better ball club."

Washington advocates interpreted Ike's remarks as a ringing endorsement of Washington baseball, but others weren't so sure. The Senators finished in last place that season, and again in 1959. They moved to Minneapolis in 1961 and became the Minnesota Twins. The team had only $25,000 in the bank when it left town, but Washington politicians raised such an outcry that a new expansion team was placed in Washington the same year.

The expansion Senators fared as poorly as their predecessors. They got a new ballpark in 1962 — D.C. Stadium, renamed R.F.K. Stadium in 1968 — but they continued to lose. In 1969 the owner, Robert Short, somehow talked the great slugger Ted Williams into managing the Senators. The team jumped to fourth place, posting a winning record for a change. Williams was named

## LOCAL HERO

■ Walter Johnson, whose magnificent career brought more baseball glory to Washington than any other player's, remains a historical figure in the area, where he put down strong roots. A public high school in suburban Bethesda, Maryland, near Johnson's former home, is named for him. The Walter Johnson plaque that was unveiled at Griffith Stadium by President Harry Truman in 1947 was moved to Walter Johnson High School when Griffith Stadium was torn down, and the 100th anniversary of Johnson's birth was observed at the school.

Johnson earned these honors with an extraordinary record. In 21 seasons, Johnson won 416 games, second only to Cy Young. He pitched 110 shutouts, more than any other pitcher in history, and his fast ball was legendary.

In retirement, Johnson got involved in politics, and was the Republican candidate for Congress from his Maryland district in 1940. (He lost the election.) He spent much of his time as a dairy farmer and loved to hunt. He died in 1946 at age 59.

Johnson and his wife had six children, most of whom still live in the Washington area.

Manager of the Year, and 918,000 fans showed up — an improvement of some 350,000 from a year before. But the Senators sagged back to last place in 1970, fans returned to other pastimes, and Short began planning a move to Dallas-Fort Worth.

Again *The Washington Post* tried to enlist the president in defense of the home team. Martie Zad, executive sports editor, wrote President Nixon: "I would like to urgently ask you for 5-10 minutes of your time to discuss your feelings about baseball in Washington. It is my hope that Shirley Povich and I might be allowed to visit with you on this matter. And from this, maybe, Shirley can do a piece that would, I'm sure, take effect in the Senators' office, the commissioner's office and around the American League."

No dice. Herbert G. Klein, the White House director of communications, dashed Zad's hopes with this reply:

"As you know, President Nixon is a great sports fan and has gone on record as being a supporter of the Washington Senators baseball team, but he feels it inappropriate to discuss their future in this city. He would certainly not want to have the nation's capital lose its major league baseball franchise. On the other hand, I am sure you can understand why it would be inappropriate for him to intercede in this business/finance matter."

Two weeks later, the *Post* reported that Nixon "had spoken with Short, and while dismayed about the prospects of losing the franchise, fully understood the circumstances and supported him." Through his press secretary, Ron Ziegler, Nixon said it would be "heartbreaking" if the Senators moved. The next day — September 21, 1971 — American League owners approved the move of the Senators to Dallas-Fort Worth. Nixon said he was "distressed," was switching his allegiance to the California Angels, and hoped to throw out the opening-day ball in Anaheim, California, the following spring. The Angels took him up on it, but Nixon had to cancel in favor of his historic trip to China in April 1972.

However, Nixon made an effort in Washington's behalf two years later. The San Diego Padres were up for sale, and Joseph Danzansky, president of a regional supermarket chain, offered to buy the franchise and move it to Washington. Nixon ran into Danzansky at a public event and offered to help. Danzansky asked the president to write a persuasive letter to Charles S. Feeney, president of the National League.

### BEST EVER

**President Truman unveils a plaque to the Senators' great pitcher, Walter Johnson, on June 21, 1947. Left to right are Edwin E. Johnson and Walter Johnson Jr., the pitcher's sons; Minnie Johnson, 82, his mother; and Edward J. Landow, who cast the plaque. Truman said, "I am honored and privileged to be called upon to unveil this plaque to a man who in my opinion was the greatest ballplayer who ever lived. He was a great ballplayer, great American, and great citizen of the United States." Walter Johnson was a Republican who campaigned for Alfred M. Landon against Franklin Roosevelt in the 1936 presidential race and ran unsuccessfully for Congress himself. Griffith Stadium, where the plaque was originally located, was torn down in 1965, and the plaque is now at Walter Johnson High School in Bethesda, Maryland, near where Johnson lived.**

Nixon obliged. "I just want to cast my own vote in favor of returning major-league baseball to the Nation's Capital," he said in a letter to Feeney dated September 7, 1973. "You can be sure all of us in the Washington metropolitan area would enthusiastically welcome a National League team."

But the Padres decided to stay put, Danzansky's financing fell short, and Washington continued to be a baseball orphan. In 1991 the National League considered Washington for an expansion team, but chose Denver and Miami instead. By then many Washington fans considered the Baltimore Orioles their home team. In 1992 the Orioles moved to a new stadium on the side of town closest to Washington and President George Bush threw out the opening-day ball. Presidents from Taft through Nixon did all they could for Washington baseball but it wasn't enough. The Senators' last manager, Ted Williams, summed up the feeling of many baseball officials about Washington when he called it a "horseshit town" with too many transients and too few home-town baseball fans.

WASHING
AMERICAN LEAGUE

BOXES

**WORLD SERIES**
**Fans line up to buy tickets for the first World**
**Series ever played in Washington — October 1924.**

JUDY LAWRY BALL

## CHAPTER XII

# The Rookie

*John F. Kennedy was an Opening Day phenom — and he always knew the score.*

A constant Kennedy family fascination was sports, and they needed scores and statistics to feed this fascination. In 1957 when John F. Kennedy was still a U.S. senator and Robert Kennedy was counsel to a Senate investigating committee, their father, Joseph P. Kennedy, pulled off a coup while in France. He got a London Sunday newspaper to agree to carry the Saturday American baseball scores. This was terribly important to Americans abroad, because the Paris edition of the New York *Herald-Tribune* carried the weekday and Saturday scores but did not publish on Sunday, leaving a

**1962 PASS**
**President Kennedy is given his American League pass on the Friday before the new District of Columbia Stadium opens. He assures (left to right) Senators General Manager Ed Doherty, Joe Cronin, president of the American League, and Elwood "Pete" Quesada, president of the Senators, that he will be at the park on Opening Day. He was.**

## NEW BOX

**President Kennedy enters the presidential box at the brand-new D.C. Stadium in Washington. The box is located next to the Senators' dugout in this, the first of the baseball-football stadiums derided as "cookie-cutters."** *Green Cathedrals* **author Philip J. Lowrey describes it as looking like "a wet straw hat, or waffle whose center stuck to the griddle because of its curved dipping roof."**

**ALL-STARS**
John F. Kennedy and Stan Musial greet
each other at the 1962 All-Star game
in Washington (the white-haired
gentleman to the left is House Speaker
John W. McCormack). Kennedy, fully
aware that Musial had campaigned for
the Democratic ticket, invited Musial
back to the White House.

## GOOD OMEN

**President Kennedy shakes hands with Senators manager Mickey Vernon while manager Bob Scheffing of the Tigers looks on. This photograph was taken in 1962, just prior to the first game ever played at the new D.C. Stadium, now called RFK Stadium. The Senators won and took temporary hold on first place in the American League.**

gap. The senior Kennedy was able to get Lord Beaverbrook, owner of the London Sunday *Express*, to promise to carry American baseball scores, a custom which has continued down to the present.

So when John F. Kennedy became president, it was not out of character for him to have an aide who was nicknamed "Undersecretary of Baseball," because he kept the president apprised of baseball scores, standings, facts and opinions during their daily White House swim.

The undersecretary of baseball was functionary Dave Powers, who not only acted as the semi-official keeper of stats and rosy Red Sox news, but as the president's ball hawk. At the ballpark Powers literally carried the president's glove. At the 1962 opener in Washington, when the Senators' Willie Tasby hit a towering foul that appeared to be headed for the president, it was Powers who tried to snag the ball. It hit the roof of the Senators' dugout, about three feet from the president, and bounced off with jet-like velocity. It hit out of reach of the lunging Powers, but it was close enough for *The Sporting News* to suggest that he "nearly earned the most valuable player award in 1962."

John F. Kennedy loved sports and sports stars. In baseball, he was fascinated with his home team, the Boston Red Sox, and with Ted Williams in particular. Kennedy became friendly with Cardinals star Stan Musial, who campaigned for the Kennedy-Johnson ticket. Kennedy saw Musial at the 1962 All-Star game and told him, "A couple of years ago they told me I was too young to be president and you were too old to be playing baseball. But we fooled them." Kennedy was forty-five at the time, and Musial was three years younger.

Known also for his cultural interests, Kennedy was able to keep things in perspective. One of his more memorable quotations reflected this balance: "Last year, more Americans went to symphonies than went to baseball games. This may be viewed as an alarming statistic, but I think that both baseball and the country will endure."

Above and beyond all of this, however, Kennedy was a great opening-day president. There were three during his short presidency, and he sat happily through all 27 innings, including a rain delay.

**April 10, 1961.** His first presidential opener was the last at Griffith Stadium. The home team was called the Washington Senators, but it was a new expansion club, the old Senators having moved to Minneapolis, where they became the Minnesota Twins. With the temperature in the upper 40s, Kennedy took off his coat and threw what was immediately termed the longest and hardest first ball ever pegged by a president. It went over the heads of the players lined up in front of the president, skipped out of one player's grasp and landed in the hands of Manuel Joseph "Jungle Jim" Rivera of the White Sox.

Rivera came over to the president's box to get Kennedy to sign the ball, as was the custom. He took one look at Kennedy's illegible signature, and according to a *Chicago Tribune* account by David Condon that appeared shortly after Kennedy's death, Rivera looked at the ball, winced and addressed the president:

"What kind of garbage college is that Harvard, where they don't even teach you to write? What kind of garbage writing is this? What is this garbage autograph? Do you think I can go into any tavern on Chicago's South Side and really say the president of the United States signed this baseball for me? I'd be run off."

Rivera drew closer to Kennedy and came to the point: "Take this thing back and give me something besides your garbage autograph."

An astonishing display of disrespect? Not really. Kennedy laughed uproariously from the start, gladly took back the ball and laboriously wrote his name on it.

Rivera was then heard to reply, "You know, you're all right."

**April 9, 1962.** Kennedy opened a spanking new $23-million ballpark in Washington, sat out a rain delay chatting with the umpires and kept a Laotian prince cooling his heels over at the White House so that he could see the whole game. He displayed his characteristic "vigah" by

## 1961 OPENER

**President Kennedy is shown with Dave Powers, his unofficial "undersecretary for baseball," who is in the middle of the group. To Powers' left is Senators general manager Ed Doherty. Behind JFK's right shoulder is White House aide Lawrence O'Brien. This was Kennedy's first opener and the last ever staged at Griffith Stadium.**

# R.F.K.

■ While no major-league park has ever been named for a president, one was named for a president's brother. The site is at 19th and North Capitol streets NE in Washington, D.C. Completed in 1962 as the District of Columbia Stadium and inaugurated by John F. Kennedy, there was an unsuccessful effort after his death in 1963 to rename it for him. The idea was spearheaded by Shirley Povich of *The Washington Post* and seconded by American League President Joe Cronin.

It was renamed, not for JFK, but for RFK. The name Robert F. Kennedy Stadium was officially bestowed on the federally-owned stadium by Interior Secretary Stewart L. Udall on the last day of Lyndon B. Johnson's presidency.

showing up topcoatless and hatless. He lit up a cigar in the eighth inning and the press seemed unanimous in their opinion that he "appeared to be thoroughly enjoying himself." At the end of the game, which the home team won 4-1, he turned to Senators president Pete Quesada and quipped, "I'm leaving you in first place."

**April 8, 1963.** Topcoatless and hatless again, he puffed on several cigars at the opener and did not have his picture taken crossing a picket line. There should have been pickets at the game because vendors at D.C. Stadium were on strike, but Secretary of Labor Willard Wirtz intervened, promising to help mediate the dispute if the president could be spared the political peril of crossing a picket line.

Besides the picket line, Kennedy had an effect on another aspect of this game: the Senators' lineup. As sportswriter Bob Addie told the behind-the-scenes story, Kennedy became interested in a rookie first baseman named Tom Brown, who had dropped out of the University of Maryland to play for the Senators. He batted .312 in spring training, creating a lot of speculation as to whether he might start at the beginning of the season.

When the Senators' general manager George Selkirk went to the White House to present Kennedy with his 1963 season pass, the subject of Brown came up. Kennedy coyly expressed regret that the rookie probably wouldn't start, but added that if he were running the club and had such a hot attraction he would start him for the lidlifter.

Selkirk brought this back to manager Mickey Vernon and Brown got the nod. He struck out three times in the opener (facing Steve Barber, who had grown up playing sandlot ball with Brown) and was soon sent back to the minors. A year later, Brown was out of baseball and on his way to becoming a fine defensive cornerback for the Green Bay Packers. Kennedy would not live to see Brown achieve success in football.

### THE TICKET
President Kennedy pleased the crowds by getting rid of his hat and overcoat for his Opening Day tosses, no matter how cold the day. Pictured here at the 1961 opener, both Kennedy and Vice President Lyndon B. Johnson opt to go coatless and hatless in the shade.

# CHAPTER XIII

# The Pride of The Pedernales

*Lyndon Johnson was the first president to dedicate a new ballpark.*

**LET 'ER FLY**
**Coattails flying, President Johnson throws out the first ball of the 1964 season. He saw the Senators lose to the Los Angeles Angels 4-0.**

**A**s president, Lyndon B. Johnson threw out the opening-day baseball three times in Washington. An opener he missed was the one that worried him. It was 1968. On March 31, Johnson addressed the nation on television about the Vietnam War. There is "division in the American house," he said, referring to widespread opposition to U.S. participation in the war. For the sake of unity, the president said, "I shall not seek and I will not accept the nomination of my party as your president."

On April 4, the Reverend Martin Luther King was shot to death in Memphis, Tennessee. King's death sparked a wave of rioting, and Washington, D.C. was among the cities affected most.

The opening of the baseball season was postponed in deference to King's funeral, then postponed again. Federal troops and the National Guard were called out in Washington. Guardsmen patrolled D.C. Stadium, home of the Senators. Soldiers bivouacked on the field.

The stadium is located in a residential area that is largely black, and fans were wary of attending. The Senators had sold 45,000 tickets for the opener, but only 32,063 fans showed up. Among the missing was President Johnson, busy with two crises — the war abroad and the strife in American cities.

Vice President Hubert H. Humphrey subbed for LBJ. Humphrey was, as usual, ebullient. "This is the finest opening day I've ever experienced," he said. The Senators were playing the Twins, from Humphrey's home state of Minnesota. Fans booed the vice president in a good-natured way, knowing he favored the Twins. "Don't worry, Cal," Humphrey told Cal Ermer, the Minnesota manager. "They're booing me, not you."

The Twins won as Dean Chance shut out the Senators, 2-0. It was the fourth Washington opening-day loss, three of them by shutouts, during the Johnson administration. National Guardsmen, wearing their fatigues and helmets in case trouble broke out, watched from the stands. One of them was Eddie Brinkman, the Senator shortstop, who had been called up with his unit.

Baseball and President Johnson were on a better footing three years before, when President and Mrs. Johnson flew to Houston to watch the first major-league game at the Astrodome, the first indoor ballpark. The game marked the first dedication of a new stadium by a president. It was only an exhibition between the Astros and New York Yankees, but a sellout crowd of 47,876 was on hand. The Johnsons got there late, so Texas Governor John Connally threw out the first ball.

**LOOK OUT, BATTER**
**The catcher in this Texas sandlot scene is Lyndon Baines Johnson, age 15.**

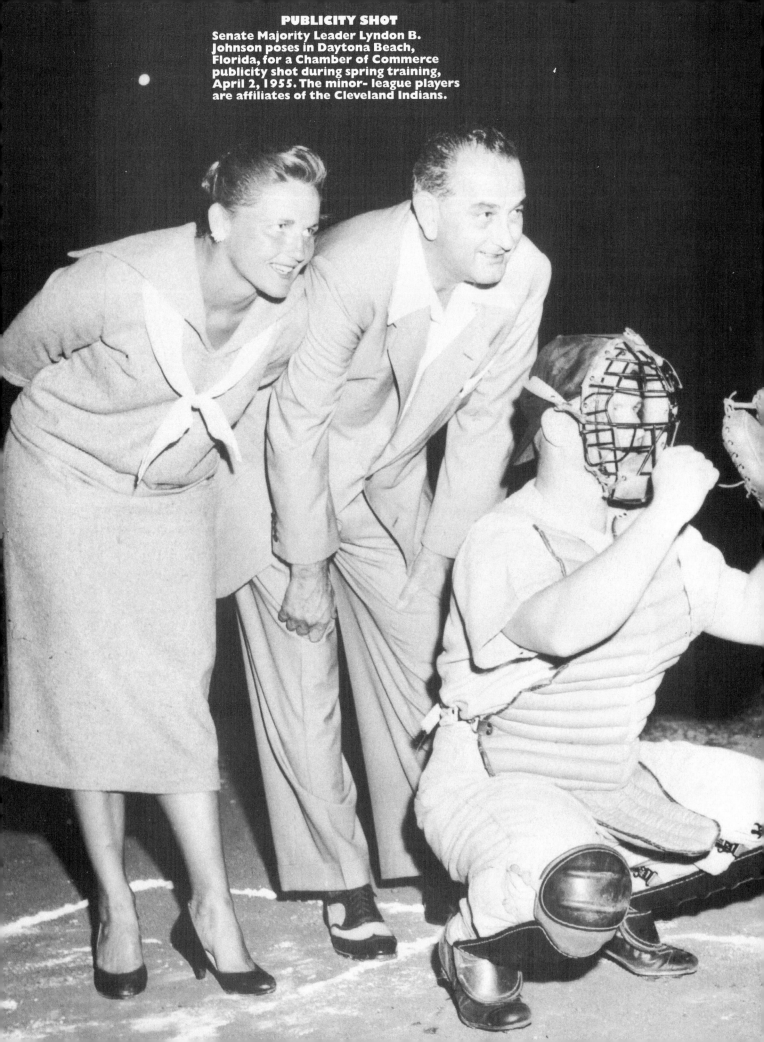

**PUBLICITY SHOT**
Senate Majority Leader Lyndon B. Johnson poses in Daytona Beach, Florida, for a Chamber of Commerce publicity shot during spring training, April 2, 1955. The minor-league players are affiliates of the Cleveland Indians.

*"They booed Ted Williams too, remember? They'll say about me I knocked the ball over the fence — but they don't like the way he stands at the plate."*

— President Lyndon B. Johnson

Mickey Mantle hit the first Astrodome homer in the sixth inning. The Johnsons left after eight innings, and Judge Roy Hofheinz, owner of the Astros and creator of the dome, set off the scoreboard's spectacular "ecstasy" display in their honor. As the Johnsons watched, the light show began with a ball bursting through the dome's ceiling, then soaring across the scoreboard. Explosions accompanied the display. Scoreboard cowboys fired ricocheting bullets of light.

The president was duly impressed. "You ought to be very proud of this stadium," he told reporters. "It is massive, beautiful, and it will be a very great asset."

During his presidency, Johnson may have thought back to the good old days, when he was just a senator and had time for baseball. Calvin Griffith, who succeeded his uncle and foster father as owner of the Senators in 1955, had this recollection for his biographer:

"Being in Washington opened up so many opportunities for you. We used to have all kinds of senators come out to the ballpark. I remember Huey Long used to be out there all the time. They used to ring this bell when they had to be back for a vote or something. Senator George of Georgia, Senator Johnson of Texas. He used to come out and eat hot dogs. I used to go out and sit with them and tell them about all these new ballplayers and who was coming. Of course that's when he was minority leader. When he became majority leader he had to change his style of living."

Aside from three opening days and the Astrodome dedication, Johnson had little time for baseball during his troubled presidency. On April 6, 1966, Commissioner William Eckert came to the White House to give Johnson his season pass, an annual ritual that presidents often used for jovial comments. Johnson allowed 30 seconds for the presentation and 30 more seconds for photographers. No questions, please. He clapped his hands and said, "Let's go. We've got a lot of work to do."

**WITH THE STARS**
**Vice President Johnson greets Whitey Ford, the Yankees' ace left-hander (left), and Stan Musial, the Cardinal slugger, at the January 13, 1961 awards banquet of the Washington Touchdown Club. Ford and Musial both received the Clark Griffith Award for their contributions to baseball, and Johnson appointed Musial to head the President's Council on Physical Fitness.**

CLEVELAND STATE UNIVERSITY

127

## POSTER BOY

**James Kaplan, 10, of Mountainside, New Jersey, gives President Johnson a baseball during a White House visit on April 2, 1968. Kaplan was the 1968 Arthritis Foundation poster boy.**

### SENATE BUDDIES

**President Johnson at the 1965 Washington opener. Behind him, left to right, are Senate Republican leader Everett McKinley Dirksen of Illinois, Senator George Smathers (D-Florida) and Senator Wayne Morse (D-Oregon).**

## POLITICIANS AT PLAY

An all-star cast of congressional heavyweights surrounds President Johnson as he throws out the first ball of the 1965 season. To Johnson's right, with a big smile, is Vice President Hubert Humphrey. Two rows behind Humphrey, also smiling, is House Republican leader Gerald Ford, and to his left, House GOP whip Leslie Arends. The elderly gentleman to Humphrey's right is House Speaker John McCormack. Senate Democratic Leader Mike Mansfield is to McCormack's right, and House Democratic Leader Carl Albert is behind McCormack's left shoulder. Senate Republican Leader Everett McKinley Dirksen, with frizzy white hair, is just behind Johnson's right shoulder. Senator Wayne Morse, with the mustache, is behind Johnson's right shoulder, and Senator Russell Long is to Morse's left. Directly behind Morse is Bill Moyers, then LBJ's press secretary, later to become a prominent television journalist. In front of Long (in profile, next to the man rubbing his eye) is Joe Cronin, president of the American League.

### PRESIDENT-TO-BE

Smiling at the opposition, President Johnson has a good word for House Republican leader Gerald Ford at the 1965 Opening Day in Washington.

## MVP

**President Johnson accepts a Carl Yastrzemski bat from the beaming Yaz, to his right, at a White House photo opportunity on January 23, 1968. As the American League's most valuable player in 1967, when he led the Boston Red Sox to their "impossible dream" pennant, Yastrzemski had been honored at a baseball writers' dinner the night before. The gent on the far right is Joe DiMaggio.**

*"We cheer for the Senators, we pray for the Senators, and we hope that the Supreme Court doesn't declare that unconstitutional."*

— Vice President Johnson, in a luncheon speech in connection with the All-Star game in Washington, D.C., July 10, 1962.

*Following page:*

### WHERE'S THE BEER?

**President Johnson shares popcorn with Congressman Leslie Arends (R-Illinois) at the 1965 opener in Washington. To Johnson's right are Vice President Hubert Humphrey and House Speaker John McCormack. Behind McCormack is House Democratic Leader Carl Albert. House Republican Leader Gerald Ford, a future president, is to Arends' left. Behind Johnson are aide Lawrence O'Brien and, looking directly into the camera as usual, Senate Republican leader Everett P. Dirksen. To Dirksen's left is Senator Wayne Morse (D-Oregon) who became an implacable foe of Johnson's over the administration's Vietnam policy.**

130

# CHAPTER XIV

# The Maven

*Richard Nixon knew so much about the game that he could have been commissioner of baseball or head of the players' union, but he ran for president instead.*

NATIONAL BASEBALL LIBRARY

**PITCHING STYLES**
**Nixon's devotion to baseball went beyond the ceremonial. When Pittsburgh star Roberto Clemente died in a plane crash on December 31, 1972 while ferrying supplies to victims of an earthquake in Nicaragua, Nixon started a Roberto Clemente Memorial Fund for earthquake victims by writing a personal check for $1,000.**

Richard Nixon has always maintained a lively, scholarly interest in baseball. His knowledge of the game probably surpasses that of any other president. He has even made use of it as an instrument of foreign policy. In 1958, on a state visit to South America, Vice President Nixon's motorcade was stoned and his car rocked by angry demonstrators in Caracas, Venezuela. He suggested that the State Department send major-league players on a goodwill mission to teach Venezuelan youngsters the finer points of baseball. The players were greeted enthusiastically, and Walter Donnelly, a former ambassador, said "that tour did more to clear the atmosphere than a dozen top-echelon conferences."

Then, in 1965, an interesting offer developed. Nixon was out of politics. He had been a congressman, a senator, and, for eight years, vice president under President Dwight Eisenhower. But then he suffered two galling defeats, to John F. Kennedy in the 1960 presidential election and to Democrat Pat Brown in the 1962 race for governor of California. "You won't have Nixon to kick around anymore," he told reporters after his 1962 defeat, and he joined a prestigious law firm in New York.

The Major League Baseball Players Association appeared to be as moribund as Nixon's political career. The "reserve clause" was still in effect, binding players to one team until traded or sold. Since a player could not quit his team without quitting baseball, team owners were able to restrain salaries and benefits. Willie Mays of the San Francisco Giants was believed to be baseball's highest-salaried player, at $105,000 annually — roughly $350,000 in 1993 dollars. That's less than one-third of the average player salary today, less than one-tenth of the top salaries.

Bob Feller, the fireballing pitching star of the Cleveland Indians, led the Players Association when it was formed in 1953. He and his colleagues worked hard to improve pension benefits. They made a little progress, but not much. By 1965 the Players Association was down to $5,400 in its treasury. It had one file cabinet, no office, no employees.

The players decided they needed a full-time director with skill and prestige. Feller was retired, and leadership of the Players Association passed to Harvey Kuenn, who was then nearing the end of his playing career, and three outstanding pitchers — Bob Friend and future Hall of Famers Jim Bunning and Robin Roberts.

*"I like the job I have now, but if I had my life to live over again, I'd like to have ended up as a sportswriter."*

– Richard Nixon

## THANKS, YAZ

**Red Sox slugger Carl Yazstrzemski — spelled "Yaztrimsky" in White House staff memos about this event — gives his 1970 All-Star game "Most Valuable Player" trophy to President Nixon as a token of respect.**

**Yaz was a man of bipartisan generosity. In 1968 he gave an urn he received as "Sportsman of the Year" to President Johnson. He also gave an engraved belt to Senator Edward Kennedy and a bat to House Speaker John McCormack. Kennedy and McCormack were both Massachusetts Democrats; Yaz was one of the most beloved Red Sox players ever.**

## ONE MORE!

Here's the opening pitch scene from the president's viewpoint. That's Richard Nixon doing the honors in Washington, with Commissioner Bowie Kuhn to his right. The White House correspondent in front of the cameraman on the far right is Dan Rather, who would later become anchor of the CBS Evening News.

**INSIDE SCOOP**
NBC's Lindsay Nelson interviews President Nixon at the 1970 All-Star game. But in 1971, White House aides disagreed on whether Nixon should grant an interview to Joe Garagiola before an upcoming World Series game. "President Nixon is a statesman and leader of the free world, not a sportscaster," said press secretary Ron Ziegler. "I think that it is an excellent idea," countered Communications Director Herb Klein. "No," said broadcast consultant John Scali, "the president is in danger of overdoing the sports fan bit." As things turned out, Nixon didn't go to the 1971 World Series, so the issue was moot.

They decided to recruit Richard Nixon, whose affinity with baseball was well known. Feller knew Nixon from World War II, when both served in the South Pacific, Feller as a gunnery leader aboard the battleship *USS Alabama* and Nixon as an officer on a communications ship. Feller recalled the situation in an interview in late 1992.

"I'm retired, so I got a call one day from Robin Roberts. He wanted me to introduce him and Bob Friend and the others to Richard Nixon, who was a lawyer in New York. Which I consented to do, and I called Nixon, who I knew from Navy days in the Marianas. I had kept in contact with him and we were very friendly.

"They wanted him to take the job as their players representative, to run the Major League Baseball Players Association. He told them he would be glad to take the job but he had political obligations so he was not in a position to do it. He offered to do the law work for them for a very reasonable amount of money."

The approach to Nixon was made by Bunning, who understood politics as well as Nixon understood baseball. After his playing career, Bunning ran for Congress and was elected from his Kentucky district.

The Players Association had to look elsewhere, and landed on their feet. They hired Marvin Miller, a veteran official of the United Steelworkers Union. Miller, a brilliant and determined negotiator, revolutionized labor-management relations in baseball. Once an arbitrator struck down the reserve clause in 1975, salaries soared.

Back to 1965, when the players weren't the only baseball faction looking for new leadership. Ford Frick, baseball commissioner since 1951, had announced his retirement. The owners heard about the players' overture to Nixon, and decided the former vice president should be their man — the new commissioner of baseball. They offered Nixon a much more prestigious job than the players could, and a much better salary — $100,000 a year plus a big expense account.

Nixon was flattered, but declined. "Don't tell Pat," he told the owners who had called on him, naming his wife. "She'd kill me for turning you down."

In looking for a second choice, the owners didn't fare as well as the players. They chose a retired Army general, William D. Eckert, whose imprint on the game was so faint that sportswriters dubbed him "the unknown soldier."

Nixon resurrected his political career, campaigning tirelessly for Republican candidates and earning the GOP nomination and election as president in 1968.

At his first Opening Day, April 7, 1969, Nixon was the victim of one error and committed another on his own. He entered the presidential box and found a misspelling on the presidential seal — "Presidnt of the United States." Then, with 60 players, managers and coaches looking on, not to mention 45,000 fans and numerous photographers, he dropped the ball he was preparing to throw. *The New York Times* called it "the first error in the 1969 season." The Washington Senators were beaten that day by the Yankees, 8 to 4, but actually finished ahead of them for the season — a rare occurrence.

### FANS NIXON AND HOOVER

Vice President Nixon and FBI Director J. Edgar Hoover cheer a Washington rally at a 1959 game. Nixon and Hoover had been close political allies since 1947, when Nixon became a member of the House Un-American Activities Committee. (Hoover's FBI provided intelligence for HUAC investigations.) For many years Nixon relied on Hoover's political counsel; Hoover advised him to make his ill-fated bid for governor of California in 1960.

### TOP FAN

Commissioner Bowie Kuhn presents President Nixon with a trophy as "Baseball's Number 1 Fan" at the 1969 White House reception. Nixon had a mixed record in backing baseball commissioners. When team owners moved to fire Kuhn in 1982, sportswriters asked former President Nixon who he thought the next commissioner should be. "The incumbent," Nixon replied. Kuhn was retained, but suspended George Steinbrenner, principal owner of the Yankees, after he was convicted of making illegal contributions to Nixon's 1972 presidential campaign. In 1992, Nixon was interviewed on ESPN during Commissioner Fay Vincent's dispute with club owners. "He seems to be a tough, strong guy, unflappable," Nixon said. "I believe baseball would make a mistake to throw him out." Seven weeks later, Vincent was out.

NIXON PROJECT, NATIONAL ARCHIVES

## HELLO, CALIFORNIA

That's Gene Autry, cow-boy-actor-turned-owner of the California Angels, with ex-president Richard Nixon at an Angels game in Anaheim, California in 1978. When the Senators left Washington following the 1972 season, President Nixon switched his allegiance to the Angels. He threw out the first ball for the Angels' home opener on April 6, 1973, sharing the honors with David Luna, a former prisoner of war in Vietnam and becoming the first president to throw out the season's first ball in another city. After resigning the presidency on August 9, 1974, Nixon did not make an appearance at a major-league ballpark until this outing four years later.

In office, Nixon was an active First Fan. He was supportive of a major-league team in Washington (see Chapter XI) and when the players went on strike in April 1972, Nixon ordered J. Curtis Counts, director of the Federal Mediation and Conciliation Service, to get the two sides together and push them toward agreement. The strike lasted just 13 days.

Richard Nixon is the only president ever to formally compile his own all-star baseball teams. He did it by eras, and the number of players and managers involved totaled 174. Although some sportswriters sniped at a few of his choices, Nixon left no doubt that he was a serious fan, whose range of baseball knowledge stretched back mightily.

How the Nixon all-star teams came to be stands as a footnote to the overriding event of the Nixon presidency: Watergate. On June 22, 1972, Nixon held his first news conference since the break-in at the Democratic National Committee five days earlier. Although the full dimensions of the crime, which included a plot to bug the headquarters, were not yet apparent, reporters were beginning to sniff out the first possible links between those arrested and the administration. Other than to denounce the break-in and to deny White House involvement, Nixon refused to answer any questions about the episode on grounds that possible criminal charges were involved.

At the conclusion of the press conference, Cliff Evans of RKO General Broadcasting asked Nixon, "Mr. President, as the nation's number one baseball fan, would you be willing to name your all-time baseball team?" Nixon, who must have been delighted at the change of subject, said he would.

Three days later, on a Sunday afternoon at Camp David in Maryland's Catoctin Mountains, Nixon tackled the project with his son-in-law, David Eisenhower, grandson of former President Dwight Eisenhower and a baseball expert in his own right. (He once served as a statistician for the Washington Senators.) While the president and his young companion whiled away the hours in the wooded retreat discussing baseball greats, his deputies and advisers back in Washington frantically searched for information about the break-in and worked to contain the political and legal fallout. For several days the president had been in almost constant contact with associates who would come to be known as key Watergate figures. In fact, the celebrated 18 1/2-minute gap occurred in a taped conversation between Nixon and H.R. Haldeman on June 20, some five days before the all-star session. Yet the president was able to turn away from the growing crisis and plunge into this labor of love.

Nixon released his team — or, to be precise, his teams — in a broadcast interview with Evans, and also wrote it up for the Associated Press. *The New York Times*, among other papers, carried the AP story under Nixon's byline, much to the disgust of its celebrated columnist, Red Smith. Noting that Nixon had expressed a desire to be a sportswriter, Smith wrote:

"Allowing the cub two or three times as much space as a staff member would get, *The New York Times* published his essay in full Sunday, all 2,800 cliche-ridden words. Frankly, the new boy has a long way to go if he's ever going to cut it in this department." (See Appendix V for Nixon's complete list.)

### CURVE BALL

**President Nixon spins the first ball at the 1970 All-Star game in Cincinnati. The Mets manager is Gil Hodges, who managed the National League All-Star team that night. Far left is David Eisenhower, Nixon's son-in-law, and his wife, Julie Nixon Eisenhower. Standing in front of the couple is Representative Robert A. Taft Jr. (R-Ohio). To the president's left is his wife, Pat, and Baseball Commissioner Bowie Kuhn. As vice president in 1959, Nixon threw out the first ball at the All-Star game in Pittsburgh, spoke at an All-Star baseball banquet, then stuck around the press room until 2 a.m., chatting with men who held jobs he claimed to covet.**

### FORK BALL?

**Richard Nixon seems to be putting something special on this flip of the ball. Nixon never claimed any prowess as a player but he was justly proud of his knowledge of and devotion to the sport. "If I had a second chance, and could choose to be a politician or go into sportswriting — not playing but writing — I would have taken writing ... I love the game, love the competition," he told ESPN's Roy Firestone on July 15, 1992.**

## CLOSE IT, TED

President Nixon wings the season's first pitch at his first presidential opener, April 7, 1969. Ted Williams, the open-mouthed manager of the Washington Senators, is flanked by a Little Leaguer and Baseball Commissioner Bowie Kuhn. Ralph Houk is the New York manager, and American League President Joe Cronin is to Houk's left.

# CHAPTER XV

# The Team Player

*Gerald Ford became a catcher for the GOP but first courted Betty while rooting for the All-American Girls Professional Baseball League.*

**PRESIDENTIAL GRIP**
**President Ford gets the ball back from catcher Jim Sundberg of the Texas Rangers after tossing it out to open the 1976 season at Arlington, Texas, on April 11.**

If you're wondering what president did the most for the feminist cause in baseball, look no further. It was Gerald R. Ford, our 38th president. After serving in the Navy during World War II, Ford returned to Grand Rapids, Michigan, where he had lived since the age of 2, and began practicing law. The All-American Girls Professional Baseball League was then in full flower, and the Grand Rapids Chicks attracted an enthusiastic local following.

When the movie "A League Of Their Own" recalled the AAGPBL in 1992, an enterprising newspaper reporter called Ford at his office in Rancho Mirage, California. Was he, by chance, a fan of the Chicks?

You bet. "I was single, practicing law," Ford recalled. "People said it was fun. Well, I went, and it sure was. The gals played hard and skillfully and put on a good show. Those ladies took it very seriously. They drew real well. Fans got very intense, and partisan. They really had a flair. It was good competition."

Ford was courting Betty Bloomer of Grand Rapids, and said he probably took her to Chicks games; he's not sure. They married in 1948, and he was elected to Congress the same year. The Chicks won the AAGPBL championship in 1953 when Beans Risinger struck out Kalamazoo's Sammy Sams with the bases loaded in the final inning of the championship game.

As president, Ford had a role in granting girls the right to play Little League baseball. The original Little League charter, signed by President Lyndon Johnson in 1964, specified that Little League was for boys. Whoa! Along came the feminist movement, followed by 22 lawsuits seeking equal opportunity for girls. Little League asked Congress to amend its charter and Congress did so, putting girls on the same footing as boys. Ford signed the bill in December 1974, four months after succeeding Richard Nixon in the White House.

During his long service in the House, Ford was a stalwart of the Republican team in the annual congressional baseball game between the Democrats and the Republicans. In 1957, first baseman Ford hit an inside-the-park grand-slam homer. (In the most recent series in this enduring classic, the Republicans hold a commanding edge: 21 to 9, with one tie.) Shortly before his death, Congressman Silvio Conte reminisced about his many years as the Republican team manager: "Over the years, I played in the congressional baseball game with the greats: Ford, Bush and Michel." Two future presidents and a minority leader singled out for what they could do between the baselines.

As vice president in 1974, Ford witnessed one of the great events in baseball history. Hank Aaron of the Atlanta Braves had hit his 713th career home run late in the 1973 season, one short of tying

## A REAL TIGER

**Ford poses with outfielder Mickey Stanley of the Detroit Tigers, in Washington to play the Senators the evening of the 1967 congressional baseball game. Ford and Stanley both hailed from Grand Rapids, Michigan.**

**LONG BALL**
House Republican leader Gerald
Ford takes a cut during the
1965 congressional game.

### THROW STRIKES

**Congressman Ford with an unidentified teammate at the annual congressional game, pitting Democrats against Republicans, on May 29, 1949. "I usually play the outfield," Ford said, "but everybody else refuses to catch so I'm stuck."**

### CHECK OUT THOSE
### CHEERLEADERS

**Ford, this time wearing a suit, with the 1967 House Republican baseball team. That's congressman and future president George Bush in the back row, third from right.**

## FAMILY GAME

Congressman Gerald Ford playing ball in 1961 with sons Jack and Mike in the back yard of their home in Alexandria, Virginia, a Washington suburb.

## BEFORE THE FALL

President Ford at the 1976 All-Star game with Pete Rose of the Cincinnati Reds and Rose's son.

148

**STEALING THEIR THUNDER**

**President Ford, flanked by Hall of Famer Hank Aaron and Commissioner Bowie Kuhn, at the 1976 All-Star game in Philadelphia. The game coincided with the Democratic National Convention in New York, giving Ford almost as much television exposure at that moment as the Democratic nominee, Jimmy Carter.**

Babe Ruth's all-time record. The Braves opened the 1974 season at Cincinnati, and Commissioner Bowie Kuhn invited Ford to accompany him to the game.

Ford threw out the first ball. Ralph Garr, the Braves' leadoff hitter, walked to open the game. The next two batters were retired, and up stepped Aaron. Jack Billingham, the Cincinnati pitcher, ran the count to 3-and-1. The crowd was on edge, anticipating the record-tying homer.

Kuhn turned to Ford and said, "This isn't a bad place for it." Aaron hit the next pitch over the head of left fielder Pete Rose and into the stands. It was his 714th homer, equaling a record that had stood for almost 40 years.

Kuhn had arranged to climb onto the field with Ford and make a presentation to Aaron, if he indeed hit the record-tying home run. But no one had informed Dick Wagner, the Reds general manager. "Nobody's going on the field," Wagner told the commissioner. "We won't interrupt the game."

Kuhn recalled the incident in his autobiography. "This was not a time for gentle persuasion," he wrote. "Gerald Ford was on his feet right behind me.

" 'Dick,' I said, 'this is very simple. The vice president is going to participate in a field ceremony right now. You have a ladder brought out, or you're suspended immediately.' We glared at one

another. Then he called for the ladder and we had the ceremony. The vice president handled it charmingly, giving no sign that he was aware of Wagner's behavior."

Ford may have been the best athlete ever to occupy the White House. At Michigan he starred at center on the football team. That's big-time college ball. Growing up in Michigan during the 1930s and '40s, he rooted for the Detroit Tiger championship teams of 1934, 1935 and 1940. In 1975 John McHale, president of the Montreal Expos and a native of Detroit, was among the baseball leaders who presented Ford with his season pass to major-league baseball games. McHale decided to test Ford's knowledge of Tiger baseball.

"Do you remember Heine Schuble, Mr. President?" McHale asked.

"Sure," Ford replied. "Wasn't he the Tigers' shortstop just before Billy Rogell?" That's as remote as trivia gets. Schuble was a Tiger regular, barely, for just two seasons.

**BAD NEWS**
**President Ford watches presidential election returns with Joe Garagiola in the White House. It was November 2, 1976, and the returns showed Democrat Jimmy Carter beating Ford. "The President took all the news very calmly," Garagiola wrote in his memoirs. "… I'd seen Enos Slaughter get more upset about an umpire saying 'Strike two' than Gerald Ford did when he realized he wasn't going to win a presidential election." Garagiola had befriended Ford after they met at a celebrity golf tournament.**

## HANK MEETS HIROHITO
At an eclectic White House reception on October 2, 1975, honoring Emperor Hirohito of Japan, Ford introduces the emperor to a reigning slugger, Hank Aaron of the Atlanta Braves. Mrs. Ford is to Hirohito's right. Mrs. Aaron is behind her husband.

# CHAPTER XVI

# The Softballer from Plains

*Jimmy Carter played softball before, during and after his presidency, and always for keeps.*

**INTENSITY**
At the plate, Jimmy Carter is at his most intense and photogenic. In this photo, taken in Plains in August 1978, Carter is in the process of beating a hometown team.

ore than 40 million Americans play softball on a regular basis — and one of them is Jimmy Carter. As candidate, president and former president, Jimmy Carter did for softball what Lyndon Johnson did for chili con carne and what Calvin Coolidge did for the Indian headdress. Softball was his great private and public indulgence. It was central. When former President Nixon tried to typify the Carter administration in 1980, he said, "They may play softball down in Plains, but they play hardball in the country."

It all began in 1976 during the presidential campaign after the Democratic Convention, when the pack of journalists following Carter found themselves at Carter's hometown of Plains, Georgia, where the candidate had gone to relax for a few days. A series of softball games commenced, pitting Carter and his crew of Secret Service agents, who called themselves the "News Makers," against a group of reporters who called themselves the "News Twisters." The media team quickly adopted a slogan — "The Grin Will Not Win." (The press had nicknamed Carter "The Grin.")

The games were great camera fodder. Carter's running mate, Senator Walter Mondale, played for the media and consumer advocate Ralph Nader umpired — in suit and tie — for one August game. At first Carter showed up in black socks and cut-offs. But after a news photograph showed Carter going up for a fly ball and displaying an unpresidential navel, he started to dress better. Soon his advisors were filming Carter at the bat for campaign television ads.

If the uniforms needed improvement, Jimmy Carter's competitive spirit did not. He took his softball seriously, always positioning himself as team captain, and played with skill. Reporters who played with him noted that Carter always knew which base to throw to. He was intolerant of lazy play.

Curtis Wilkie, White House correspondent for *The Boston Globe*, related this anecdote to *Sports Illustrated*: "One time I was playing third base on Carter's team and someone hit a pop fly in my direction. It was well out of my range, but I gave it a little chase anyway. When I got back to third base, he was standing there staring at me, and he said, 'You should have had that one, Curtis.' I never knew if he was serious or not."

One player said Carter's teammates included "bionic Secret Service men," including a shortstop who had played triple-A ball. "All of the Secret Service guys were terrified that if they messed up they might end up stationed in Ohio," he said.

153

## UNDERHANDED

**President Jimmy Carter displays his form as a slow-pitch twirler in a Plains, Georgia, game in September 1979. Carter, a direct man in politics, brought deception to his position as pitcher.**

154

**BROTHER BILLY**

**The younger Carter swings and misses during a softball game in Plains in 1978. The First Brother was a great softball lover and sometimes captained the president's team during his absences.**

## NO FREE LUNCH

■ Every president from Teddy Roosevelt on participated in the annual photo opportunity in which baseball leaders call on the president, present him with a season pass and exchange words about the great and continuing traditions that link baseball with every phase of American life. But not Jimmy Carter.

According to James Fitzpatrick, a lawyer representing organized baseball, overtures were made for then-Commissioner Bowie Kuhn to bring Carter his pass for the 1977 season. Word came back that the new president would take a pass on the pass, because he was not doing things in the traditional manner. After all, he had begun his presidency by *walking* back from his inauguration.

Fitzpatrick argued that this was a time-honored ritual. An appointment was finally scheduled, and Kuhn and Fitzpatrick went to the White House — where they were ushered to the basement. There Carter's son Chip accepted the pass for his father.

155

**CONCENTRATION**

**At the plate, Jimmy Carter fiercely focuses on the ball. Here he goes for a high pitch in an August 1978 game with a hometown team.**

Five days before Carter took office, the Atlanta Braves made a visit to Plains. Carter ate barbecue with owner Ted Turner and hobnobbed with the players and coaches, but begged off a softball game to work on his inaugural speech. He let Billy Carter pitch to Hank Aaron and other Braves, past and present. Nobody was supposed to keep score; but Aaron revealed that it was Braves 4, Billy Carter's All-Stars 3.

Carter's softball wasn't just for campaigning. As president, he visited Plains in August 1978, teamed up with his Secret Service detail and beat a local team led by his brother 6-5. Once out of office, Carter and his former White House associates played a media team captained by television newscaster Sam Donaldson on August 31, 1985.

"You may think that this is for fun, but this is a grudge match," said Donaldson. "In 1976 Jimmy Carter got the Secret Service on his team and they consistently beat the media, but today he has just bums like us."

The game was a rough one. An attempt to push Donaldson off second base so that he could be tagged out was foiled when Donaldson picked up the base and clutched it in his arms.

Carter's team prevailed, but only with the help of a ringer. With the former president's team down 5-4, he went to his bench for a special player who produced a game-winning home run. She

## THE OTHER IKE

**President Carter and Milton Eisenhower, president of Baltimore's Johns Hopkins University, after Eisenhower threw out the first ball for the seventh game of the 1979 World Series.**

## CARTER ON ATHLETICS

■ "I was on the varsity basketball team in high school and, when I was in submarines, I was the pitcher on our baseball team. I learned there, obviously, that you have to be mutually dependent to achieve an identifiable goal, and you have to learn how to accept either defeat or victory with some degree of equanimity and look to the next contest with hope and anticipation. I think you have to yield sometimes your own selfish aspirations for the common good and be able to deal with one another in an open, sometimes competitive way, but not a personally antagonistic way. I think those are some of the lessons that you learn from team sports and I hope that I remember them."

— Jimmy Carter as Democratic presidential nominee, quoted in the *Los Angeles Times*, August 24, 1976.

### D.C. GOES TO BALTIMORE
**Although it was the only major-league game he attended as president, Carter was not the only politician at the seventh game of the 1979 World Series in Baltimore. Also chatting with Commissioner Bowie Kuhn is House Speaker Thomas P. "Tip" O'Neill.**

was 19-year-old DeAnn Young of Plains, who hit 23 homers for Georgia Southwestern College that spring. Even Republicans celebrated this use of a ringer to humble the self-assured Donaldson.

Carter had problems with baseball. It was almost as if he was coached in baseball ineptitude, as if he had been brought up someplace where the game is not part of the social fabric. When he finally attended a major-league game, it was game seven of the 1979 World Series in Baltimore. The witty and irrepressible Rick Dempsey, Oriole catcher, on seeing the president in the edgy Orioles' clubhouse, said in a voice that could be heard by his teammates and a few reporters, "Next time, get your ass here before the seventh game." The Orioles lost to the Pirates and a few in Baltimore still think the president was, to use the phrase of William Howard Taft, a hoodoo who jinxed the Washington team on his first trip to the ballpark.

During the game, sitting in a box with Speaker of the House Thomas P. "Tip" O'Neill and Baseball Commissioner Bowie Kuhn, Carter put his finger on it. As Kuhn put it in his memoir *Hardball*, Carter told him that he was more interested in playing sports than in watching them. As Kuhn wrote later, "Since one of the those participatory sports was softball, I could be forgiving."

Carter was still to have one great baseball moment, at another postseason seventh game. He was in Atlanta in October 1992 for Francisco Cabrera's ninth-inning, two-out game-winning shot that put the Braves over the Pirates 3-2 and into the World Series. It was one of the great moments in the history of the game and Carter acted appropriately. He jumped over the box seat railing, dodged police horses and hugged players and coaches.

**LOCKER ROOM TALK**
The president looks on as Willie Stargell of the Pittsburgh Pirates and Don Drysdale, broadcaster and former Dodger star, say hello in the Pirates locker room before the seventh game of the 1979 World Series in Baltimore.

# CHAPTER XVII
# The Pitch Man

*Baseball took Ronald Reagan to Hollywood; Hollywood took him back to baseball and on to the White House.*

t was one of the president's favorite stories, and no one tired of hearing it. Young "Dutch" Reagan was broadcasting a Chicago Cubs game over station WHO in Des Moines, Iowa, on an afternoon in the mid-1930s. He worked from a telegraphic report. An operator handed him curt accounts of each pitch and each play: "Strike one," or "popped out to second." Reagan re-created the game by making up the details that bring a ball game to life for radio listeners.

It was the ninth inning of a scoreless game between the Cubs and the St. Louis Cardinals. Dizzy Dean was pitching for the Cards; Augie Galan was the Cubs' batter. Using his fertile imagination, Reagan described Dean's windup and the first pitch. The operator handed him a slip saying "The wire has gone dead."

THE SPORTING NEWS

*Yours For Kentucky Winners and Kentucky Club
Dutch Reagan*

**DAPPER DUTCH**
Ronald Reagan, star sportscaster for WHO, Des Moines, Iowa, in the 1930s. The picture may have been taken for a pipe tobacco advertisement. The inscription at the bottom reads, "Yours for Kentucky Winners and Kentucky Club. Dutch Reagan."

161

## THE RIGHT-HANDER

**President Reagan winds up to throw out the first ball of the 1986 season at Baltimore Memorial Stadium. Orioles owner Edward Bennett Williams is just behind Reagan; Commissioner Peter Ueberroth is to the president's left.**

**OUCH!**
Reagan in a down moment of Grover Cleveland Alexander's career, when he pitched for the Chicago Cubs. "Making this picture was as happy a chore as I'd had since playing the 'Gipper,'" Reagan recalled, alluding to his famous role in "Knute Rockne, All-American."

**CUBS REUNION**

**President Reagan, who broadcast Chicago Cubs games in the 1930s, greets Ernie Banks, "Mr. Cub," at the White House on March 27, 1981. Banks was one of 32 Hall of Famers who lunched with the president that day.**

## TIP'S TALE

■ As speaker of the House, Thomas P. "Tip" O'Neill had several important antiques in his office, including a desk that had once belonged to President Grover Cleveland. He has a favorite story about that desk concerning the day that Ronald Reagan noticed it. O'Neill was recently prevailed upon to retell the story:

"He had just been inaugurated as president of the United States and he was using the Speaker's Lounge and the speaker's men's room to change his clothes. He's in this formal dress and he wants to change into business clothes to go to the luncheon. He's sitting over there [by the desk] and says, 'Hey, Grover Cleveland. I played him in the movies.'

"I sez no. You played Grover Cleveland Alexander, the baseball player. And then I knew the nation was in tough shape from that moment on. But a good, lovable guy."

165

## OLD RADIO GUY

**President Reagan joins Cubs announcer Harry Caray in the broadcast booth at Chicago's Wrigley Field on September 30, 1988, during a political swing. Reagan called an inning and a half of action. "You know, in a few months I'm going to be out of work and I thought I might as well audition," the president said. "You could tell he was an old radio guy," Caray said. "He never once looked at the television monitor."**

**OLD-TIMERS**
**Harmon Killibrew (left) gives President Reagan an autographed ball at the White House luncheon for Hall of Famers. Warren Spahn is partially hidden by Reagan.**

"I had a ball on the way to the plate and there was no way to call it back," Reagan wrote in his memoirs. "... So I had Augie foul this pitch down the left field foul line .... He fouled for six minutes and forty-five seconds .... My voice was rising in pitch and threatening to crack — and then, bless him, Curly started typing. I clutched at the slip. It said: 'Galan popped out on the first ball pitched.'"

Reagan began his sportscasting career at WHO in 1932 shortly after graduating from Eureka (Illinois) College, where he played football but not baseball. He was nearsighted. "I never cared for baseball ... because I was ball-shy at batting," he recalled. "When I stood at the plate, the ball appeared out of nowhere about two feet in front of me. I was always the last chosen for a side in any game. Then I discovered football: no little invisible ball — just another guy to grab or knock down, and it didn't matter if his face was blurred."

The young sportscaster was hired to broadcast football games of the University of Iowa Hawkeyes. Baseball was added to his menu when WHO signed on to re-create Cubs games.

**SIGNING UP**

**President Reagan signs a proclamation designating May 1983 as National Amateur Baseball Month. The uniformed players are the Athletes and Dodgers, Pony League teams from Glen Burnie, Maryland, who played an inning of baseball on the South Lawn of the White House right after the May 11, 1983 Rose Garden ceremony. That's Stan Musial standing just to the president's right.**

Reagan had never seen a big-league baseball game. He traveled to Chicago, watched a few games from the Wrigley Field press box, took instruction on telegraphic re-creation, and went on the air in Des Moines.

He was a hit. In 1936 *The Sporting News* ran a write-in poll asking readers, "Who Is Your Favorite Baseball Broadcaster?" Among broadcasters working in cities not in the major leagues, Reagan finished fourth. *The Sporting News* pictured him as "An Iowa Air Ace," and credited him with "a thorough knowledge of the game, a gift for narrative and a pleasant voice."

Reagan was 25. The Cubs trained back then on Catalina Island, California, and Reagan was sent west to cover spring training in 1937. He was developing Hollywood aspirations, and he had a connection through a barn dance group called the Oklahoma Outlaws, who did a regular show on WHO. The Outlaws had been hired by Gene Autry to play in one of his westerns. Reagan called on their agent, whom he knew through WHO, and the agent got him an audition at Warner Brothers.

The woman in charge of selection for Warner watched Reagan's takes and said: "He's the greatest find since Robert Taylor — if he'll just get rid of those glasses and do something about that awful haircut."

## STRIKEOUT
**Frank Lovejoy (right) as Rogers Hornsby hands the ball to Ronald Reagan for his big moment in "The Winning Team," the story of pitcher Grover Cleveland Alexander's life. Alexander was epileptic, but the movie did not disclose his illness. Doris Day played Mrs. Alexander.**

He did, and his heart was no longer with the Cubs, though he still had to cover spring training. "One day on Catalina, Charlie Grimm, the Cubs' manager, bawled me out for not even showing up at the practice field," Reagan recalled. "How could I tell him that somewhere within myself was the knowledge I would no longer be a sports announcer?"

Reagan starred in a number of roles. By 1950 his acting career was winding down, but Warner Brothers picked him to play Grover Cleveland Alexander, the great pitcher, in the 1952 movie "The Winning Team." He was engaged to Nancy, an avid baseball fan, and she was enthralled by the film's extras — big leaguers Gene Mauch, Hank Sauer, Chuck Stevens, Peanuts Lowery, Jerry Priddy, Johnny Berardino and Bob Lemon.

"I was the player that plunked Reagan with a ball between the eyes as he was heading for second," recalled Lowery. "We used a cotton ball. And when I hit him I shouted, 'Look out!' But the director said, 'Cut!' He figured I would get an extra $350 for having a speaking role. So we reshot the scene, and after I hit Reagan, I had to look sad and keep my face down as Reagan was sprawled on the ground."

169

Bob Lemon, the great Cleveland Indians pitcher, was Reagan's tutor and double. "He was very graceful and easy to teach," Lemon said of Reagan. "I had this little quirk in my own motion where I did a little hop after I released the ball so I would be in position to field a ball hit back at me. By the time they started shooting the movie, Reagan was doing exactly the same thing."

The movie's most dramatic scene re-created the seventh game of the 1926 World Series, when the Cardinals' Alexander, 39 and weary from pitching a complete-game victory the day before, relieved in the seventh inning and struck out the Yankees' Tony Lazzeri with the bases loaded. Lazzeri was played by Johnny Berardino, a journeyman infielder who played for the St. Louis Browns, Cleveland Indians and Pittsburgh Pirates, and had acting aspirations of his own. Berardino later dropped the second "r" in his name and achieved success as Dr. Steve Hardy, a leading character in the soap opera "General Hospital."

"The Winning Team" burnished the fame that helped propel Reagan into politics. He was elected governor of California in 1966, served two terms, was elected president in 1980 and reelected in 1984, both times in landslides.

He didn't forget baseball. On March 27, 1981, Reagan hosted a White House luncheon for 32 retired baseball stars. Reagan sat between Duke Snider and Willie Mays, and reminisced. "Nostalgia bubbles within me and I might have to be dragged away," he said. The players were impressed. "I think the president enjoyed this visit even more than we did," Joe DiMaggio said.

Three days later Reagan was shot and wounded outside a Washington hotel where he had just delivered a speech. The president had been scheduled to throw out the first ball of the All-Star game in Cincinnati April 8. No one substituted; the crowd observed a moment of silence instead.

Silence wasn't characteristic of Reagan, at least not for long. On July 12, 1989, six months after leaving the presidency, Reagan joined Vin Scully in the broadcast booth at the All-Star Game in Anaheim, California. Jimmy Reese, the California Angels coach who once roomed with Babe Ruth, threw out the game's first ball, so Scully invited Reagan to "throw out the first adjective."

Reagan was 78, and there was little left of the bright young broadcasting star for WHO, Des Moines. One critic, Pete Coutros of the *New York Post*, wrote, "Somewhere along the way — it's been some distance — the man who loomed so invincible on celluloid had lost his stuff. On Tuesday night, all Ronald Reagan had left was his change of pace."

For most viewers, it was enough — still Reagan, still baseball.

**HONORARY TWIN**
Frank Viola, star left-hander for the world champion Minnesota Twins, presents Reagan with a Twins shirt at a White House ceremony October 29, 1987. That's Kent Hrbek, the Twins slugger, in the rear behind Reagan's left shoulder. Steve Carlton, wearing sunglasses, is next to Hrbek. Howie Fox, a Twins official, is just to Reagan's right. Tom Kelly, the Twins manager, is at the podium.

# CHAPTER XVIII

# The Natural

*George Bush was a Yale glove man who kept his mitt in his White House desk drawer.*

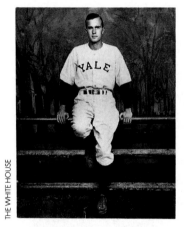

**MISTER BASEBALL**
**George Bush in his Yale uniform. The future president was the stalwart first baseman on a team that reached the finals of the College World Series two years in a row. In one of those finales, Bush was in the on-deck circle when a triple play killed the Elis' final rally.**

They booed George Bush at the 1992 All-Star Game in San Diego, California, United States of America. The Associated Press said he was, in fact, "roundly booed" and noted that even having his friend Ted Williams with him didn't help. Heck, they were still booing him when he turned to chat with Willie Mays, the honorary National League captain for the evening.

Bush took it well. He surely knew that baseball fans booed President Hoover (protesting Prohibition, not to mention the Depression) and President Harry Truman (over the firing of General MacArthur). In fact, Bush resigned himself to this possibility when still vice president. "Normally, they boo politicians at baseball parks; that kind of goes with the territory," he said in April 1986. As president, he admitted to sportswriter Tom Boswell that in 1988 he avoided the possibility of being booed in Cincinnati by taking the field with an 8-year-old girl and a 12-year-old boy. "I said to the little girl, 'Are you nervous? ... Why don't we walk out together'. ... It was a little defensive on my part," Bush confessed to Boswell, "but it worked."

But to boo this fellow in a ballpark is almost akin to booing the pope in church. Bush was baseball's buddy, a good player and the guy who may have uttered the ultimate presidential testimonial to the game. When asked why he was fascinated with baseball, he replied: "It's just got everything."

Bush was born with a real baseball tradition. His father, Prescott Bush, batted cleanup on the 1917 Yale team while also playing on the golf team. His mother hit a softball home run in Kennebunkport the day his older brother (also named Prescott) was born. After circling the bases, she announced that it was time to go to the hospital. Growing up, he dreamed of owning Lou Gehrig's mitt, rooted for the Red Sox and saw plenty of games at Yankee Stadium and the Polo Grounds. He caught a foul ball at Yankee Stadium.

Back from World War II in 1945, Bush entered Yale, where he started at first base for the varsity team. He did not miss a baseball game for two seasons, while going through Yale's four-year program in just two and one-half years.

Those were tough postwar teams, and his Yale teammates included three men who went to the majors. What Poppy (his nickname) lacked at the plate — Bush batted .239 in 1947 and .264 in 1948 — he made up for as a sure-gloved first baseman.

## BUSH AND THE BABE

**The captain of the Yale nine receives a signed copy of Babe Ruth's memoirs from the great Yankee star in 1948, months before Ruth's death. Ruth had been on campus to present the manuscript of the memoirs to the Yale library. Bush brought the Babe over to meet his teammates before they began that day's game.**

**RIP & POPPY**
**Two baseball kinda guys: Cal Ripkin Jr. of the Baltimore Orioles and the president. Both Ripkin and Bush had less than spectacular seasons in 1992 — although Ripkin at least kept his job.**

## THE MOMENT THEY STARTED CALLING HIM "FIRST FAN"

■ Q: The delay of baseball's opening day is imminent. Is there anything that you as the "First Fan" can do — (laughter) — to bring the sides closer together to prevent a tragic delay of the baseball season ... ?

A: Yes, I'm a ball fan and I want to go to the opening game someplace. Last year I went to the American League. This year I would like to go to the National League, if possible. I don't know whether it's going to work, maybe going to end up in Baltimore.

But I want to see — I don't want to intervene ... I would simply appeal to both sides to get the matter resolved so the American people can hear that cry, "Play ball," again ....

— Press conference, March 13, 1990, on the impending lockout.

**MULTINATIONAL**
President George Bush and Canadian Prime Minister Brian Mulroney double up for an April 1990 Canadian opener in Toronto. In 1992, Bush became the first U.S. president during whose term a Canadian team, the Toronto Blue Jays, won the World Series.

### BUSH ARTIFACTS
**George Bush's baseball memorabilia, displayed at the Richard Nixon Library and Birthplace in Yorba Linda, California, during the summer of 1992.**

A teammate, Dick Tettlebach, who went on to play for the Yankees and Senators, compared him to Keith Hernandez. Tettlebach told Tom Boswell of *The Washington Post* that Bush was "Absolutely superb. A real fancy Dan." His old coach, Ethan Allen, called him "a one-hand artist at first base," alluding to the fact that he did not catch with two hands, which was still the way most infielders worked. Poppy threw left, batted right. And Bush was enough of a leader that his teammates made him captain of the 1948 team.

The Yale team was at the top of the college pyramid. The 1947 College World Series was the first ever, and Yale reached the final game, losing to the University of California on a home run blast by Jackie Jensen, who went on to star for the Red Sox. Yale reached the final game again in 1948, this time losing to Southern California.

Jensen was not the only future star Bush encountered in spikes and baggy pants. The other first baseman in a game against the University of Connecticut was soon-to-be Rookie of the Year Walt Dropo. A guy named Vin Scully was the 1947 Fordham center fielder, and football great Glenn Davis played center field for Army. USC's batboy in the 1948 championship game was a 14-year-old kid named George "Sparky" Anderson.

Bush was involved defensively in a triple play against Amherst in April 1948, but almost didn't score from second against Trinity when he collided with his own third-base coach.

Was there a moment at which he thought he might play professionally? In 1991 he told *Sports Collectors Digest*: "Once after an especially strong day at bat in a game at Raleigh, N.C., I was 3-for-5 with a double and a triple, and a scout approached me as I left the field. That was the first

175

Captain of championship college baseball team, while completing college in 2½ years after war service. Phi Beta Kappa— Economics.

**SCHOLAR-ATHLETE**
George Bush in his Yale uniform, with a yearbook description of his achievements as an Eli.

**SOFTY**
President Bush winds up with a softball in a display of glovesmanship. During his time in office, he kept his Rawlings-George McQuinn trapper in a desk drawer in the Oval Office.

and last nibble I ever got from the pros." That game against North Carolina State, incidentally, was written up in the Raleigh *News and Opinion* and talked of Bush as "Yale's husky first sacker."

Bush also had a moment at Yale which linked him forever with the man who is still the dominant figure in baseball. Ravaged with cancer and only months from death, Babe Ruth went to New Haven in 1948 to present the Yale library with the manuscript copy of *The Babe Ruth Story*. As Yale captain, Bush accepted the manuscript from the Bambino in a ceremony staged just before the Yale-Princeton baseball game. Years later Bush recalled what Ruth said to him as he handed him the book: "You know when you write a book like this, you can't put everything in it."

Just before postseason play got underway in October 1989, Bush invited ten sports reporters and broadcasters to the White House to talk baseball. He recalled his old Yale coach, Ethan Allen, and his lifetime big-league batting average (1926 through 1938) of exactly .300. He told stories about his pals Bart Giamatti, who had died on September 1st, and the new commissioner Fay Vincent. Bush was never far from baseball. He kept a *Baseball Encyclopedia* next to his desk and his original 1945 George McQuinn/Rawlings "Claw" mitt in his desk.

Bush may have been our most eager first-ball pitcher, a role that culminated in his opening the 1992 season at the new Oriole Stadium at Camden Yards in Baltimore with a single pitch from the mound.

Not all of his first balls were good. As vice president he bounced a ball in the dirt in the Astrodome.

After that bouncer, he sought advice from Nolan Ryan, the great pitcher. "Nolan says throw it high because amateurs get out there, no matter how good they are, and throw it into the dirt," Bush recalled. "You get more of an 'ooooh' [from the crowd] if you heave it over the [catcher's] head instead of going with the fast-breaking deuce into the dirt."

Perhaps the grandest baseball moment of Bush's adult years came when he was vice president. It showed that he was still a player, not just an old man heaving a ball on Opening Day.

In a 1985 interview with M. Charles Bakst of *The Providence Journal*, Bush described the event, which took place in 1981 in Denver. The veep had given a press conference, and a group of former players in town for an old-timers game asked Bush if he'd like to play that night. He suited up and was taken to the ballpark in an unmarked car. The crowd learned of the surprise player when he was announced as a pinch hitter. He popped up against Warren Spahn, then was given a turn against Milt Pappas.

"Pappas grooved one and I hit it — I hadn't swung a bat, in, God, how many years! — I hit it crisp right through the middle for a single .... People actually cheered and stuff when I got the single. It was more fun!"

But there was more. After returning to the dugout, the old-timers insisted that he play first base for an inning.

"I said 'Play? Good God, I don't think I could even see the ball coming across!' I did have my glasses, and so they gave me a mitt, a brand-new first baseman's mitt. I'm a left-hander. Went out there. The first guy grounded out. The shortstop threw him out: I managed to catch the ball all right. We got another guy — somehow there was another out."

Then the moment. Forty-four-year-old Tony Oliva came to bat and the other infielders convinced their 57-year-old first baseman to move back to the grass. They maintained that Oliva could still hit and, sure enough, he pulled one down the line.

"Went to my left," Bush told the *Journal*, "Knocked the ball down. I should have had it clean. And Pappas comes across and covers first and we threw him out and the place was really thrilled with me!"

## ANOTHER PRESIDENT BOOED
Ted Williams and George Bush team up at the 1992 All-Star game in San Diego. The crowd booed Bush: was it the economy or the fact that the president and his party tied up traffic?

# CHAPTER XIX

# The Cards-Turned-Cubs Fan

*Bill Clinton grew up in Arkansas listening to St. Louis Cardinals games on the radio but a girl from Chicago persuaded him to switch loyalties.*

**CAMPAIGN CATCH**
**Governor Bill Clinton of Arkansas, campaigning for president, catches a ball thrown by Art Howe, manager of the Houston Astros, at the Astros spring training camp in Kissimmee, Florida, March 9, 1992.**

As a boy, Bill Clinton, like Harry Truman, was a musician, not a ballplayer. Truman played the piano, Clinton the saxophone. Both were good at it. But Clinton liked following major-league play and did so through the vast radio network of the St. Louis Cardinals. He grew up rooting for the Cards teams of Stan Musial and Red Schoendienst. Then he married a Chicago girl. Hillary Rodham Clinton was a fan of the Cubs, an ancient arch-rival of the Cardinals. Cable television brought Cubs games to Arkansas, and somehow Hillary Clinton persuaded her husband to switch his allegiance.

As president, Clinton took on a task tougher than any pennant race—the players' strike, which began August 12, 1994, and forced the cancellation of the World Series for the first time in ninety years. As the 1995 season approached, the team owners and the players' union were still at loggerheads. Clinton ordered the two sides to resume bargaining, and he set a deadline of February 6, 1995, for progress to have been made in the negotiations. The baseball negotiators ignored him, so Clinton summoned both sides to the White House for a negotiating session. A former labor secretary, William J. Usery, drew up a proposed compromise, but the players rejected it. Clinton and Vice President Al Gore met in the White House Cabinet Room with negotiators for both sides, including slugger Cecil Fielder, then of the Detroit Tigers, pitching aces Tom Glavine of the Atlanta Braves and David Cone, then of the Kansas City Royals, and shortstop Jay Bell of the Pittsburgh Pirates.

Presidential pressure didn't work. The players and owners were so inflexible that they rarely spoke to one another, instead addressing their comments to Clinton and Gore. Clinton asked Congress to pass legislation that would impose binding arbitration. "I have done all I could to change this situation," Clinton said. ". . . Clearly, they are not capable of settling this strike without an umpire." But House Speaker Newt Gingrich and Senate Majority Leader Bob Dole refused, saying government should stay out of private management-labor disputes.

In a subsequent interview, Clinton said he was "in a slump" on the issue. He said "personal hard feelings" between the negotiators impeded progress and correctly predicted that attendance would suffer once play resumed. "Along the way they're going to lose millions of more American fans who will just get fed up with

## CAMPAIGN MUFF

**Bill Clinton just misses a pop fly in a pickup softball game during a campaign stop in Ontario, California, July 26, 1992. Clinton is the second straight southpaw president, and the 1992 campaign matched three left-handers — Clinton, George Bush and Ross Perot.**

## CUBS FAN

**Hillary Rodham Clinton throws out the first ball of the season at Wrigley Field as the Chicago Cubs open their 1994 schedule against the New York Mets. Mrs. Clinton was the first First Lady accorded that honor. Illinois Governor Jim Edgar is to Mrs. Clinton's left.**

it," the president said. Former president Jimmy Carter chimed in, calling the impasse "disgusting" and offering to mediate. His offer, too, was declined. Play finally resumed April 25, 1995, with baseball's old economic system still in place. A year and a half later, owners and players finally consummated a new contract.

Clinton and his wife, Hillary, shared happier experiences as softball fans during their years in Little Rock, Arkansas when their daughter, Chelsea, played in the Hillcrest Softball League. Clinton was a busy governor, but he attended most of the games. Mrs. Clinton, as wife of the governor, usually threw out the first ball of the season.

During Clinton's first presidential campaign, in 1992, the Hillcrest League's volunteer officials doubted that Mrs. Clinton would show up for opening day; she, too, was campaigning. But they mailed her an invitation just in case, and she took a break from the campaign to fulfill her pleasant opening-day assignment. As she tossed the first pitch, the public address announcer said, "Next year we're going to throw out the first ball on the lawn of the White House."

## GOOD ARM

**President Clinton, followed by Baltimore Mayor Kurt Schmoke, waves to the crowd at Oriole Park at Camden Yards before throwing out the opening day pitch on April 5, 1993. Clinton, who had warmed up prior to the toss, threw a strike from the pitcher's mound to the Oriole catcher.**

App

# Major League Games Attended by Presidents in Office

*(and the Washington Openers They Missed)*

U.S. NEWS COLLECTION, THE LIBRARY OF CONGRESS

**1966 — At D.C. Stadium, Vice President Hubert H. Humphrey prepares to throw out one of the two Opening Day pitches he tossed as a stand-in for President Johnson. The managers with HHH are, left, Birdie Tebbetts of Cleveland and Gil Hodges of the Senators.**

*Preceding pages:*

**1916 — Woodrow Wilson and the second Mrs. Wilson show the world that they enjoy a spring afternoon at the ballpark.**

The bulk of this list was compiled by L. Robert Davids, founder of the Society for American Baseball Research.

Season openers that the presidents attended and threw out the first ball are starred.

## Benjamin Harrison

June 6, 1892, at Washington. Saw part of the National League game where Cincinnati defeated the Senators 7-4 in 11 innings.

June 25, 1892, at Washington. Senators lost to Phillies 9-2. Ed Delahanty hit a home run in the third.

## William Howard Taft

April 19, 1909, at Washington. Arrived in second inning as Senators lost to Boston 8-4.

May 29, 1909, at Pittsburgh. Cubs won 8-3 in 11 innings at Exposition Park.

September 16, 1909, at Chicago. Giants beat the Cubs 2-1.

*April 14, 1910, at Washington. Threw out the first ball in the first presidential opener. Walter Johnson beat the Athletics 3-0 in 1-hitter.

May 4, 1910, at St. Louis. Saw only two innings as Cards beat Reds 12-3.

May 4, 1910, at St. Louis. Browns tied Cleveland 3-3 in 14 innings. Taft saw last part of game in visit to both St. Louis parks.

May 10, 1910, at Pittsburgh. Some 8000 fans crowded the gates before the game, anxious to see the president make his entry. A crowd of 20,265 — a big turnout back then — joined Taft in watching the Pirates beat the Cubs 5-2.

May 24, 1910, at Washington. Senators beat Detroit 3-2 in rain-shortened game.

May 26, 1910, at Washington. Senators lost to Tigers 5-1. He shook hands with Detroit players.

*April 12, 1911, at Washington. Threw out first ball at opener and Boston lost.

September 23, 1911, at St. Louis. Cardinals beat Phillies 5-2.

May 7, 1912, at Cincinnati. Phillies beat Reds in Taft's hometown.

June 18, 1912, at Washington. Threw out first ball as Senators beat Athletics 5-4. It was their 17th victory in a row.

August 13, 1912, at Washington. White Sox beat the Senators 5-3.

*Opener missed:*

April 19, 1912, at Washington. The *Titanic* disaster prevented Taft from attending. Vice President Sherman threw out the first ball and saw Washington beat Philadelphia 6-0.

## Woodrow Wilson

*April 10, 1913, at Washington. Threw out first ball in opener as Johnson beat the Yankees 2-1.

April 22, 1913, at Washington. Wilson attended the first of three games in a row. The Boston Red Sox won 8-3.

April 24, 1913, at Washington. Red Sox won again, 6-3.

April 25, 1913, Washington. Senators finally beat Red Sox 5-4.

May 29, 1913, at Washington. Senators beat Red Sox 5-2.

August 2, 1913, at Washington. Senators beat Detroit 3-2 on "Walter Johnson Day."

July 14, 1914, at Washington. Detroit beat Washington 2-0.

*April 14, 1915, at Washington. Threw out first ball in opener as Johnson beat N.Y. Yankees 7-0.

October 9, 1915, at Philadelphia. The first president to attend a World Series, Wilson threw out the first ball of the second game where the Red Sox beat the Phillies 2-1.

*April 20, 1916, at Washington. Threw out first ball at home opener; Senators beat Yankees 12-4.

May 24, 1918, at Washington. Threw out first ball at Red Cross benefit. The Senators battled the Tigers to a 2-2 tie in 16 innings.

*Openers missed:*

April 23, 1914, at Washington. Speaker of the House Champ Clark threw out the first ball. Boston won 5-0.

April 20, 1917, at Washington. Vice President Marshall threw out first ball and Philadelphia won 6-0.

April 15, 1918, at Washington. For this wartime opener, District Commissioner Louis Brownlow tossed inaugural ball. New York won 6-3.

April 23, 1919, at Washington. At another wartime opener, General Match, Army chief of staff, threw out first ball. The Senators squeezed out a win against Philadelphia, 1-0.

April 22, 1920, at Washington. Vice President Marshall substituted at this opener and Washington beat Boston 8-5.

## Warren Harding

*April 13, 1921, at Washington. Threw out first ball; Red Sox beat Senators in opener 6-3.

*April 12, 1922, at Washington. Threw out first ball and this year the Senators beat the Yankees at the opener 6-5.

May 22, 1922, at Washington. Senators lost to White Sox 4-3.

April 24, 1923, at New York. Babe Ruth hit a home run and the Yankees won 4-0.

*April 26, 1923, at Washington. Threw out first ball at home opener. Philadelphia won 2-1.

## Calvin Coolidge

*April 15, 1924, at Washington. Threw out first ball at opener as Johnson beat Philadelphia Athletics 4-0.

June 26, 1924, at Washington. Threw out ball at second game of twin bill. Philadelphia won 1-0.

October 4, 1924, at Washington. Threw out first ball at first game of World Series. Giants beat Senators 4-3 in 12 innings.

October 9, 1924, at Washington. Attended sixth game of World Series. Senators beat Giants 2-1.

October 10, 1924, at Washington. Senators won final game of World Series 4-3 in 12 innings.

*April 22, 1925, at Washington. In home opener, Senators beat Yanks 10-1.

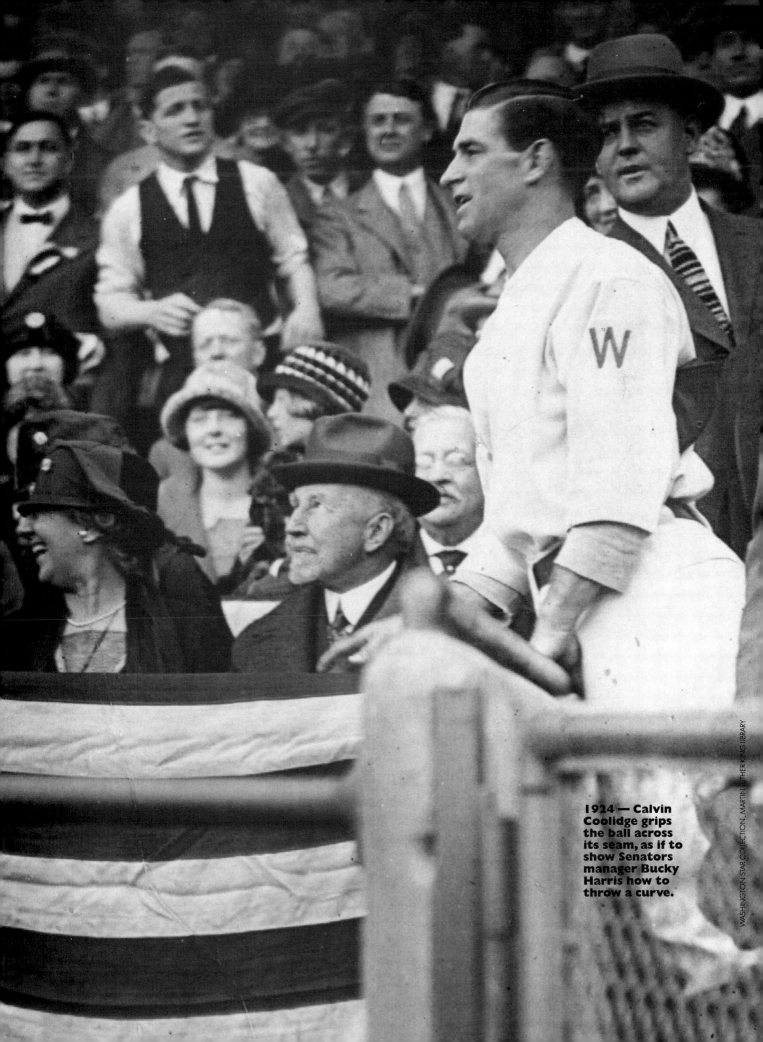

1924 — Calvin Coolidge grips the ball across its seam, as if to show Senators manager Bucky Harris how to throw a curve.

June 18, 1925, at Washington. Presented the Senators' Walter Johnson with the 1924 Most Valuable Player trophy before a game with the Browns. Coolidge left during the first inning.

October 4, 1925, at Washington. Threw out first ball of third game of the World Series. The Senators beat the Pirates 4-3.

*April 12, 1927, at Washington. Threw first ball of opener; the Senators beat the Red Sox 6-2.

*April 10, 1928, at Washington. Again threw first ball, but this time Boston won 7-5.

*Opener missed:*

April 13, 1926, at Washington. Vice President Dawes substituted; Washington beat Philadelphia 1-0.

## Herbert Hoover

*April 17, 1929, at Washington. Threw out first ball of opener. Philadelphia Athletics won 13-4.

October 14, 1929, at Philadelphia. Attended final game of World Series. Athletics beat the Cubs 3-2.

*April 14, 1930, at Washington. Threw out first ball of opener. Red Sox won 4-3.

July 30, 1930, at Washington. Final score Athletics 7, Senators 4.

October 1, 1930, at Philadelphia. Attended first game of World Series. The indomitable Athletics beat the Cardinals 5-2.

April 14, 1931, at Washington. Threw out first ball of opener. The Athletics won again, this time 5-3.

July 7, 1931, at Washington. Athletics beat the Senators 7-3.

October 5, 1931, at Philadelphia. Attended third game of World Series. This time the Cards beat the Athletics 5-2.

*April 11, 1932, at Washington. Threw out first ball at opener. Washington beat the Red Sox 1-0 in 10 innings.

## Franklin Roosevelt

*April 12, 1933, at Washington. Threw out first ball at opener. Senators beat Athletics 4-1.

October 5, 1933, at Washington. Threw out first ball at third game of World Series. Earl Whitehill shut out the Giants 4-0.

*April 24, 1934, at Washington. Threw out first ball at home opener. Boston won 5-0.

*April 17, 1935, at Washington. Threw out first ball at opener. Senators beat Athletics 4-2.

*April 14, 1936, at Washington. Threw out first ball at opener. Washington topped New York Yankees 1-0.

October 2, 1936, at New York. Threw out first ball at third game of World Series. Yankees beat Giants 18-4.

*April 19, 1937, at Washington. Threw out first ball at opener. Athletics won 4-3.

July 7, 1937, at Washington. The first president to attend an All-Star game tossed out the first ball. Lou Gehrig led American League to 8-3 win.

*April 18, 1938, at Washington. Threw out first ball at opener. Senators beat Athletics 12-8.

*April 16, 1940, at Washington. FDR threw out first ball at opener, and smashed camera of a *Washington Post* photographer. Red Sox won 1- 0.

*April 14, 1941, at Washington. Threw out first ball at opener. Yankees won 3-0.

*Openers missed:*

April 21, 1939, at Washington. New York beat Senators 6-3. Vice President Garner threw out first ball.

April 14, 1942, at Washington. Vice President Wallace threw the first ball and New York beat Washington 7-0.

April 20, 1943, at Washington. For this war-time opener, Manpower Commissioner Paul McNutt threw out the first ball and Washington beat the Athletics 7-5.

April 18, 1944, at Washington. Again Vice President Wallace substituted; Athletics beat the Senators 3-2.

## Harry Truman

September 8, 1945, at Washington. Now that WWII was over, the president could go back to the ballpark. Truman threw out the first ball and the Senators defeated the Browns 4-1.

*April 15, 1946, at Washington. The first left-handed president threw out the first ball at opener. Boston Red Sox won 6-2.

June 1, 1946, at Washington. Senators beat the Tigers 5-3.

*April 18, 1947, at Washington. Threw out first ball at opener. Yankees win 7-0.

June 21, 1947, at Washington. A monument to the late Walter Johnson was dedicated and the Senators beat the Browns 5-4.

*April 19, 1948, at Washington. Threw out first ball at opener. New York Yankees won 12-4.

August 17, 1948, at Washington. The first president to see a night game witnessed the ignominious defeat of the Senators by the Yankees, 8-1.

*April 18, 1949, at Washington. Threw out first ball at opener. Senators beat Athletics 3-2.

May 14, 1949, at Washington. Senators beat Red Sox 5-4.

*April 18, 1950, at Washington. The president threw out two first balls, one right-handed, one left. Senators topped Athletics 8-7.

August 29, 1950, at Washington. Senators beat the Tigers 5-4 in a night game.

*April 20, 1951, at Washington. Threw out first ball of Senators' home opener. They defeated the Yanks 5-3.

September 1, 1951, at Washington. In a re-creation of the World Series of 1924, Truman threw out the first ball and the Yankees won 4-0.

*April 15, 1952, at Washington. Threw out first ball at opener. Red Sox won 4-0.

July 4, 1952, at Washington. The first president to attend a ballgame on Independence Day saw the Yankees win 9-4.

July 5, 1952, at Washington. This time the Senators beat the Red Sox 4-3.

*Opener missed:*

April 20, 1945, at Washington. In this last war-time opener, Sam Rayburn threw out the first ball and New York beat the Senators 6-3.

## Dwight Eisenhower

*April 16, 1953, at Washington. Due to a golfing date, Eisenhower would have missed the April 13th opening day. However, it was rained out, and he did attend the re-scheduled Opening Day game of the 16th. New York beat Washington anyway, 6-3.

*April 13, 1954, at Washington. Threw out first ball at opener. Senators beat Yankees 5-3 on Mickey Vernon's home run in the 10th inning.

May 27, 1954, at Washington. The Senators beat the Yankees 7-3 on Red Cross Day.

*April 11, 1955, at Washington. Threw out first ball at opener. Senators beat Baltimore Orioles 12-5.

*April 17, 1956, at Washington. Threw out first ball at opener. New York Yankees took it 10-4.

August 31, 1956, at Washington. Yankees won a night game 6-4. Jim Lemon hit three home runs for the Senators.

October 3, 1956, at Brooklyn. Attended first game of World Series. Dodgers beat Yankees 6-3.

*April 15, 1957, at Washington. Threw out first ball in opener. Orioles won 7-6 in 11 innings.

July 30, 1957, at Washington. Cleveland beat the Senators soundly in a night game, 7-1.

*April 14, 1958, at Washington. Threw out first ball in opener. Washington beat Boston Red Sox 5-2.

May 29, 1959, at Washington. Senators beat Red Sox 7-6.

*April 18, 1960, at Washington. Threw out first ball at opener. Senators beat Red Sox 10-1.

August 15, 1960, at Washington. Red Sox won night game 11-3.

*Opener missed:*

April 9, 1959, at Washington. Vice President Nixon gladly substituted in throwing out first ball. Washington beat Baltimore 9-2.

## John Kennedy

*April 10, 1961, at Washington. Threw out first ball at the first opener for the expansion-team Senators. Chicago White Sox won 4-3.

*April 9, 1962, at Washington. Threw out first ball at inauguration of the new D.C.

1948 — President Truman lets one fly at Griffith Stadium. The managers are Joe Kuhel of the Senators, who would wind up in seventh place, and Bucky Harris — frequent and former Nats manager — of the Yankees, who finished 2 $\frac{1}{2}$ games behind Cleveland. Bess Truman is seated to her husband's right. House Speaker Joseph Martin, the president's GOP foe, is seen under his arm.

Stadium in Washington. Senators beat Detroit 4-1.

July 10, 1962, at Washington. Threw out first ball at All-Star game. National League team won 3-1.

*April 8, 1963, at Washington. Threw out first ball at opener. Orioles won 3-1.

## Lyndon Johnson

*April 13, 1964, at Washington. Threw out first ball at opener. Los Angeles Angels won 4-0.

April 9, 1965, at Houston. This exhibition game between the Astros and the Yankees was for the dedication of the Astrodome. The home team took it 2-1.

*April 12, 1965, at Washington. Threw out first ball at opener. Boston Red Sox won 7-2.

*April 10, 1967, at Washington. Threw out first ball at opener. Yankees won 8-0.

*Openers missed:*

April 11, 1966, at Washington. Vice President Humphrey threw out the first ball and Cleveland beat the Senators 5-2.

April 10, 1968, at Washington. Humphrey substituted again and the team from his home state, the Twins, beat the Senators 2-0.

## Richard Nixon

*April 7, 1969, at Washington. Threw out first ball at opener. Yankees won 8-4.

June 11, 1969, at Washington. Oakland won the night game 6-4 in 13 innings.

June 19, 1969, at Washington. The Orioles won the night game 2-0; Nixon didn't show up until the eighth inning.

July 9, 1969, at Washington. The Senators defeated the Indians in a night game 3-0.

July 15, 1969, at Washington. Senators beat Detroit in another night game, 7-3. The Tigers made a triple play.

April 6, 1970, at Washington. The opening game, but the president didn't arrive until the fifth inning, so Nixon's son-in-law David Eisenhower threw out first ball. Detroit drubbed Washington 5-0.

July 14, 1970, at Cincinnati. Threw out the first ball at first All-Star game played at night. National League won 5-4 in 12 innings.

July 20, 1970, at Washington. Senators beat Milwaukee 2-0 in night game.

July 26, 1970, at Anaheim. The Angels defeated the Senators 11-10 in an 11-inning Sunday game.

July 20, 1971, at Washington. Senators beat Milwaukee 6-2 in night game.

*April 6, 1973, at Anaheim. Shared honor of throwing out first ball with Major Luna, returned prisoner of war, at Angels opener. Angels beat Kansas City 3-2.

*Opener missed:*

April 5, 1971, at Washington. M/Sgt. David Pitzer, a former prisoner of war in Vietnam, threw out the first ball. Washington beat Oakland 8-0.

## Gerald Ford

April 9, 1976, at Arlington, Texas. Threw out first ball of the season for the Texas Rangers, who beat the Minnesota Twins 2-1 in 11 innings behind Gaylord Perry. Ford missed the action, leaving in the first inning.

July 13, 1976, at Philadelphia. In the bicentennial year, participated in the All-Star game festivities. Threw ball right-handed to National League catcher Johnny Bench and left-handed to American League catcher Carlton Fisk. The National League won 7-1.

## Jimmy Carter

October 17, 1979, at Baltimore. Attended last game of the World Series, won by Pittsburgh 4-1.

## Ronald Reagan

October 11, 1983, at Baltimore. Declined opportunity to throw out first ball of first game of World Series for security reasons. Left after seven innings. Phillies won 2-1.

April 2, 1984, at Baltimore. Evidently changed mind about security: Threw out first pitch at Orioles opener and sat in dugout. White Sox won 5-2.

April 7, 1986, at Baltimore. Threw out first pitch at Orioles opener. Indians won 6-4.

September 30, 1988, at Chicago. Threw out two ceremonial first pitches. Broadcast $1^1/_2$ innings on radio, then departed after the third. Missed the best part, since the Cubs lost to the Pirates 10-9 in 10 innings.

## George Bush

April 3, 1989, at Baltimore. Threw out first ball at Orioles' opener. They beat the Red Sox 5-4. Cal Ripken hit a 3-run homer off Roger Clemens.

April 25, 1989, at Anaheim. Threw out first ball. Orioles won 8-1.

June 28, 1989, at Baltimore. Threw out first ball in 2-1 win over Blue Jays.

August 4, 1989, at Baltimore. Texas beat Orioles 6-4.

April 10, 1990, at Toronto. The first president to attend a major-league game in Canada joined Prime Minister Brian Mulroney in throwing out the first balls of the Blue Jays opener. Toronto beat Texas 2-1.

July 16, 1990, at Baltimore. Threw out first ball. Orioles beat Texas 7-6.

April 8, 1991, at Arlington, Texas. Threw out first ball at Rangers opener. Texas lost to Milwaukee 5-4.

May 15, 1991, at Baltimore. The president took Queen Elizabeth to Memorial Stadium for two innings of the Orioles-Oakland A's game.

April 6, 1992, at Baltimore. The president's 15-year-old grandson, George P. Bush, joined him in throwing out the first balls as the Orioles defeated the Indians 2-0 in the new stadium at Camden Yards.

July 14, 1992, at San Diego. Bush joined Ted Williams in throwing out the first ball of the All-Star game, won by the American League 13-6.

## Bill Clinton

April 4, 1993, at Baltimore. From the pitcher's mound at Camden Yards, threw out the first ball of the season and watched the Texas Rangers beat the Orioles 7-4.

April 4, 1994, at Cleveland. Threw out the first ball of the season to inaugurate Jacobs Field. The President was accompanied by Ohio Governor George Voinovich and Cleveland Mayor Mike White. The Indians beat the Seattle Mariners 4-3 in 10 innings.

September 6, 1995, at Baltimore. Clinton and Vice President Albert Gore joined a full house at Camden Yards to watch the Orioles' Cal Ripken play in his 2,131st consecutive game, breaking Lou Gehrig's record. It marked the first time a president and vice president attended a big-league game together outside Washington.

April 2, 1996, at Baltimore. Threw out the first ball of the season at Camden Yards. The Orioles beat the Kansas City Royals 4-2.

1961 — John F. Kennedy, observed by a passel of political notables, tosses the last first ball ever tossed at Griffith Stadium.

# F.D.R.'s Baseball In-Basket

Some Americans think the president of the United States is the commander-in-chief of baseball, with sundry powers over the game.

The papers of every president reveal a remarkable array of baseball-related stuff — scores of requests for signed baseballs, sponsorship of teams, testimonials, special favors and ballpark dedications. In Franklin D. Roosevelt's papers, for example, a few letters in the 1930s addressed significant matters, including requests for his support in sending American teams to Japan. These requests sparked the president's interest and support, but seem to have died from lack of money rather than lack of approval. As late as the fall of 1940, an old United Press reporter named Henry Misslewitz was trying to raise $100,000 to create a Pacific League including Japan and ensuring "peace through baseball."

Some letters are remarkably odd or quaint, ranging from a man who wants Roosevelt to adopt his revolutionary new scoring system to a group of kids who voluntarily include their fingerprints with their request for free uniforms.

Here is a small and select sampling with paraphrases of the White House responses:

A 1934 request for the president to sign a testimonial to Babe Ruth [*OK, but no publicity stunts*]

A 1935 proposal from a group of boys who would be glad to name their team the N.R.A. Eagles in return for White House sponsorship [*Sorry fellas, but no*]

A 1936 request from the Washington Elite Giants of the Negro Southern League for the president to throw out the opening ball [*Thanks for the offer, but the president is too busy*]

A 1936 request for use of the president's pass while he is in Canada [*No response*]

A 1936 letter from the Synod of the Reformed Presbyterian Church of North America objecting to his "disregard of the sacredness and rest of the Lord's Day," evidenced by several Sunday press briefings and a baseball game in New York [*OK, but he does go to church*]

A 1937 letter from a distillery asking for permission to decorate the presidential box for opening day [*Outside White House control*]

A request by *The Sporting News* for Roosevelt to award Lou Gehrig a gold watch at the 1937 All-Star game [*Denied*]

A request to sign a 1938 petition which would change the eligibility rules for students playing in the D.C. high schools. [*No*]

A 1939 request that the president send an autographed baseball to a boy who lost his legs in a railroad accident [*Yes*]

A 1939 scheme to create an immense baseball covered with a presidential proclamation concerning the game. It would travel around the nation and be signed by fans. [*No*]

**TRUE FAN**
FDR at a game in Washington, April 18, 1938.

A 1941 telegram from the Brooklyn First Committee to the president: "UNLESS YOU ATTEND BROOKLYN DODGERS PARADE THIS MONDAY BROOKLYN WILL SECEDE FROM THE UNION." [*Filed with no answer*]

The volume of letters continued after Pearl Harbor, but requests had a new edge:

A 1942 wire suggesting that the first baseball thrown by the president be labeled "First Offensive Ball" and auctioned to the highest bidder, to benefit Defense Bonds [*File and forget*]

A 1944 letter nominating Ford Frick of the National League to succeed Judge K.M. Landis on his retirement [*President does not appoint*]

A 1943 postcard telling the president "Don't Let Hitler Kill Baseball." [*Filed*]

A 1943 letter from a Toledo man arguing for a "Black and White All Star Classic" as a step towards "The day when Negro baseball players will be permitted to play beside the White man in the major leagues." [*Ignored*]

A 1943 request from Congressman John McCormack of Massachusetts to get Ted Williams excused from military duty to play in a charity game in Boston. [*Denied*]

A 1944 note from one Chester Adelberg asking to be made new commissioner on retirement of Judge Landis. [*Filed*]

# Walter Johnson's Presidential Record

Walter Johnson, the greatest pitcher of his era and perhaps the greatest of all time, almost always opened the season for the Senators, which meant that he starred at the major leagues' official Opening Day. For the statistically minded, take in the following:

Johnson pitched seven openers with the president of the United States in attendance.

He pitched before presidents four times on other than opening days.

As manager of the Senators, Johnson took part in four presidential Opening Day ceremonies.

He managed in two other games that were not openers but at which presidents were present.

The Senators played 21 games before presidents at which Johnson was neither pitching nor managing but was a member of the team.

As a spectator or journalist (after his career Johnson covered a few games as a broadcaster or writer) he was on hand for six games at which presidents were in attendance.

All told, Walter Johnson and one president or another attended 44 games together.

The 44 games broken down by president:

*Woodrow Wilson* . . 11 games
*Calvin Coolidge* . . . 9
*Herbert Hoover* . . . 8
*William Taft* . . . . . . 7
*Warren Harding* . . 5
*Franklin Roosevelt* . 4

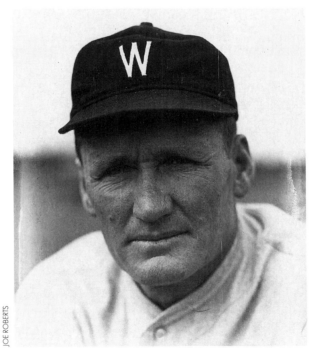

JOE ROBERTS

**HIMSELF**
**Walter "Big Train" Johnson, pitcher extraordinaire.**

# Stengel Speaks Out

What is the point of a book that talks about baseball and politics, and does not reserve a page for this exchange between Senator William Langer (R-N.D.) and manager Casey Stengel at a 1958 Senate hearing on the need for baseball antitrust legislation?

*Senator Langer:* I want to know whether you intend to keep on monopolizing the world's championship in New York City?

*Mr. Stengel:* Well, I will tell you. I got a little concern yesterday in the first three innings when I saw the three players I had gotten rid of, and I said when I lost nine what am I going to do and when I had a couple of my players I thought so great of that did not do so good up to the sixth inning I was more confused but I finally had to go and call on a young man in Baltimore that we don't own and the Yankees don't own him, and he is doing pretty good, and I would actually have to tell you that I think we are more the Greta Garbo type now from success.

We are being hated, I mean, from the ownership and all, we are being hated. Every sport that gets too great or one individual — but if we made 27 cents and it pays to have a winner at home, why would you have a good winner in your own park if you were an owner? That is the result of baseball. An owner gets most of the money at home and it is up to him and his staff to do better or they ought to be discharged.

Following the testimony from the 68-year-old "Perfessor," Mickey Mantle was called as a witness and asked if he had any "observations with reference to the applicability of the antitrust laws to baseball."

"My views are just about the same as Casey's," Mantle replied.

NIXON PROJECT, NATIONAL ARCHIVES

**THE OL' PERFESSOR**
President Nixon talks baseball with Casey Stengel, long-time manager of the New York Yankees, at the White House. It was July 22, 1969, and Nixon was hosting Stengel, some three dozen other all-time greats, about 60 active players and other members of the baseball establishment at the White House, in honor of organized baseball's 100th anniversary. "Like many who have never made the team, I am awed by those who have made it," Nixon told the players. "I'm proud to be in your company." Ted Williams, a strong Nixon supporter, skipped the party because he objected to dressing up. Another informally inclined Hall of Famer was pitcher Lefty Grove, whom Commissioner Bowie Kuhn found lounging on one White House antique with his feet on another.

# Dick Nixon's A*l*l-S*t*a*r*s

Richard Nixon's all-star, all-time baseball teams date back to 1925, when he began following the game. They represent one fan's opinion of who the greatest players were at different positions in different eras. Experts disagreed with some of the selections but acknowledged that they have stood up pretty well. Nixon's teams reveal an intimate familiarity with major-league history, lore and records.

Nixon picked his first all-stars in 1972, with the help of his son-in-law, David Eisenhower. [See Chapter XIV.] In 1992, again with Eisenhower's assistance, he updated his choices and reorganized his periods of play to reflect the 20 years of play and players since the first selections.

Jackie Robinson, the first African-American to play in the major leagues, was named by Nixon as baseball's greatest all-around athlete. (Robinson had starred during his college years at UCLA in football, basketball, golf and track.) Among other players Nixon saw in action, he cited Ted Williams as the greatest hitter, Joe DiMaggio as the best outfielder, Brooks Robinson as the best infielder and Sandy Koufax as the best pitcher.

Nixon's 1972 selections generated plenty of friendly publicity at the time, which didn't hurt the president's re-election campaign that year. Nor did the thank-you notes, and occasional expressions of political support, that came to him from some of the players who made his teams. One was from Jackie Robinson, who had supported Nixon's candidacy in 1960. (Tragically, less than four months later Robinson was dead from diabetes and heart disease.) Another was from Dick Groat, Pirates hero of the 1960s. Groat and Nixon knew each other independent of either's stardom; Groat had roomed at Duke with Nixon's brother Ed. During Nixon's 1968 campaign for the presidency, Groat co-chaired the Allegheny County (Pennsylvania) Sports Committee for Nixon.

In 1992, the Richard Nixon Presidential Library and Birthplace in Yorba Linda, California, mounted an exhibit on presidents and baseball, borrowing photos and memorabilia from the Hall of Fame in Cooperstown, New York, and from presidential libraries. The featured event was a luncheon July 15 at which the 79-year-old Nixon presented his updated version of his all-time teams. The affair was co-hosted by former baseball commissioner Peter Ueberroth, California Angels owner Gene Autry and Dodgers Manager Tommy Lasorda, among others.

A number of the old-timers chosen by Nixon were on hand, including Maury Wills, the base-stealing Dodgers shortstop of the

*Preceding pages:*

**TIGER STARS**
**President Nixon and Vice President Gerald Ford, a Detroit fan, greet Tigers stars Mickey Stanley, Joe Sparma and Al Kaline at the White House, July 15, 1969. During his presidency, Nixon wrote more than 25 letters of congratulation or condolence to ballplayers.**

1960s; Bob Feller, the great Cleveland Indians pitcher of the 1930s and '40s; sluggers Johnny Mize of the Cardinals and Giants and Harmon Killibrew of the Senators and the Minnesota Twins; and Brooks Robinson of the Orioles.

For his updated teams, Nixon broke history into what he called the Yankee Era from 1925 through 1959, the Expansion Era from 1960 through 1991, and currently active players as of 1992.

# THE 1972 NIXON DREAM TEAM
## AMERICAN LEAGUE * EARLY ERA 1925-45

|  |  | |  |  |
|---|---|---|---|---|
| First Base | Lou Gehrig | | Pitcher | Red Ruffing |
| Second Base | Charlie Gehringer | | Pitcher | Bobo Newsom |
| Third Base | Red Rolfe | | | |
| Shortstop | Joe Cronin | | *Reserves* | |
| Outfielder | Babe Ruth | | | |
| Outfielder | Joe DiMaggio | | Infielder | Jimmie Foxx |
| Outfielder | Al Simmons | | Infielder | Hank Greenberg |
| Catcher | Mickey Cochrane | | Infielder | Luke Appling |
| Catcher | Bill Dickey | | Outfielder | Goose Goslin |
| Pitcher | Satchel Paige | | Outfielder | Harry Heilman |
| Pitcher | Herb Pennock | | Relief Pitcher | Johnny Murphy |
| Pitcher | Lefty Grove | | Manager | Connie Mack |

## NATIONAL LEAGUE * EARLY ERA 1925-45

|  |  | |  |  |
|---|---|---|---|---|
| First Base | Bill Terry | | Pitcher | Mort Cooper |
| Second Base | Rogers Hornsby | | Pitcher | Burleigh Grimes |
| Third Base | Pie Traynor | | | |
| Shortstop | Arky Vaughan | | *Reserves* | |
| Outfielder | Paul Waner | | | |
| Outfielder | Mel Ott | | Outfielder | Ducky Medwick |
| Outfielder | Hack Wilson | | Infielder | Frankie Frisch |
| Catcher | Ernie Lombardi | | Outfielder | Chuck Klein |
| Catcher | Gabby Hartnett | | Infielder | Marty Marion |
| Pitcher | Carl Hubbell | | Outfielder | Edd Roush |
| Pitcher | Dizzy Dean | | Relief Pitcher | Mace Brown |
| Pitcher | Bucky Walters | | Manager | Branch Rickey |

## AMERICAN LEAGUE * MODERN ERA 1945-70

|  |  | |  |  |
|---|---|---|---|---|
| First Base | Harmon Killebrew | | Pitcher | Whitey Ford |
| Second Base | Nellie Fox | | Pitcher | Dave McNally |
| Third Base | Brooks Robinson | | | |
| Shortstop | Lou Boudreau | | *Reserves* | |
| Outfielder | Ted Williams | | | |
| Outfielder | Mickey Mantle | | Outfielder | Al Kaline |
| Outfielder | Frank Robinson | | Infielder | Bobby Richardson |
| Catcher | Yogi Berra | | Infielder | Luis Aparicio |
| Catcher | Elston Howard | | Outfielder | Carl Yastrzemski |
| Pitcher | Bob Lemon | | Outfielder | Tony Oliva |
| Pitcher | Bob Feller | | Relief Pitcher | Hoyt Wilhelm |
| Pitcher | Early Wynn | | Manager | Casey Stengel |

## HEAVY-HITTING VOTERS

President Nixon, up for reelection in 1972, welcomes three supporters to the White House. From left to right are Bobby Thomson, Mrs. Babe Ruth, Nixon and Ralph Branca. Thomson homered off Branca in "the shot heard 'round the world" that gave the New York Giants the 1951 pennant over Branca's Brooklyn Dodgers. Although once rivals, Thomson and Branca said, "now we are united in our views on President Nixon's continued leadership in the country." Nixon's aides tried to contact Mrs. Lou Gehrig for the same photo opportunity but couldn't locate her.

> "I never leave a game before the last pitch, because in baseball, as in life and especially in politics, you never know what will happen."
>
> — President Richard M. Nixon

|  |  |  |  |
|---|---|---|---|
| First Base | Stan Musial | Pitcher | Bob Gibson |
| Second Base | Jackie Robinson | Pitcher | Robin Roberts |
| Third Base | Eddie Mathews | | |
| Shortstop | Ernie Banks | *Reserves* | |
| Outfielder | Hank Aaron | | |
| Outfielder | Willie Mays | Infielder | Maury Wills |
| Outfielder | Roberto Clemente | Infielder | Dick Groat |
| Catcher | Roy Campanella | Outfielder | Duke Snider |
| Catcher | Johnny Bench | Infielder | Willie McCovey |
| Pitcher | Sandy Koufax | Infielder | Ken Boyer |
| Pitcher | Warren Spahn | Relief Pitcher | Roy Face |
| Pitcher | Juan Marichal | Manager | Walter Alston |

# THE 1992 NIXON DREAM TEAM

## THE YANKEE ERA * NATIONAL LEAGUE TEAM 1925-59

|  |  |  |  |
|---|---|---|---|
| First Base | Johnny Mize | Designated | |
| Second Base | Jackie Robinson | Hitter | Rogers Hornsby |
| Third Base | Ed Mathews | Pitcher | Carl Hubbell |
| Shortstop | Ernie Banks | Pitcher | Dizzy Dean |
| Outfielder | Stan Musial | Pitcher | Warren Spahn |
| Outfielder | Willie Mays | Pitcher | Robin Roberts |
| Outfielder | Mel Ott | Pitcher | Elroy Face |
| Catcher | Roy Campanella | Manager | Branch Rickey |

## THE YANKEE ERA * AMERICAN LEAGUE TEAM 1925-59

|  |  |  |  |
|---|---|---|---|
| First Base | Lou Gehrig | Designated | |
| Second Base | Charlie Gehringer | Hitter | Jimmie Foxx |
| Third Base | George Kell | Pitcher | Lefty Grove |
| Shortstop | Phil Rizzuto | Pitcher | Bobo Newsom |
| Outfielder | Babe Ruth | Pitcher | Bob Feller |
| Outfielder | Joe DiMaggio | Pitcher | Early Wynn |
| Outfielder | Ted Williams | Pitcher | Satchell Paige |
| Catcher | Mickey Cochrane | Manager | Casey Stengel |

## THE EXPANSION ERA * NATIONAL LEAGUE TEAM 1960-91

|  |  |  |  |
|---|---|---|---|
| First Base | Willie McCovey | Designated | |
| Second Base | Joe Morgan | Hitter | Pete Rose |
| Third Base | Mike Schmidt | Pitcher | Sandy Koufax |
| Shortstop | Maury Wills | Pitcher | Juan Marichal |
| Outfielder | Henry Aaron | Pitcher | Bob Gibson |
| Outfielder | Lou Brock | Pitcher | Steve Carlton |
| Outfielder | Roberto Clemente | Pitcher | Tom Seaver |
| Catcher | Johnny Bench | Manager | Walter Alston |

## THE EXPANSION ERA * NATIONAL LEAGUE TEAM 1960-91

|  |  |  |  |
|---|---|---|---|
| First Base | Harmon Killebrew | Designated | |
| Second Base | Bobby Grich | Hitter | Rod Carew |
| Third Base | Brooks Robinson | Pitcher | Catfish Hunter |
| Shortstop | Luis Aparicio | Pitcher | Jim Palmer |
| Outfielder | Carl Yastrzemski | Pitcher | Whitey Ford |
| Outfielder | Mickey Mantle | Pitcher | Luis Tiant |
| Outfielder | Reggie Jackson | Pitcher | Rollie Fingers |
| Catcher | Thurmon Munson | Manager | Billy Martin |

## ACTIVE PLAYERS AS OF 1992 * NATIONAL LEAGUE

|  |  |  |  |
|---|---|---|---|
| First Base | Will Clark | Designated | |
| Second Base | Ryne Sandberg | Hitter | Bobby Bonilla |
| Third Base | Howard Johnson | Pitcher | Dwight Gooden |
| Shortstop | Ozzie Smith | Pitcher | Bret Saberhagen |
| Outfield | Tony Gwynn | Pitcher | David Cone |
| Outfield | Darryl Strawberry | Pitcher | Rob Dibble |
| Outfield | Andre Dawson | Pitcher | Lee Smith |
| Catcher | Gary Carter | Manager | Tommy Lasorda |

## ACTIVE PLAYERS AS OF 1992 * AMERICAN LEAGUE

|  |  |  |  |
|---|---|---|---|
| First Base | Don Mattingly | Designated | |
| Second Base | Roberto Alomar | Hitter | Jose Canseco |
| Third Base | George Brett | Pitcher | Nolan Ryan |
| Shortstop | Cal Ripken, Jr. | Pitcher | Jack Morris |
| Outfielder | Rickey Henderson | Pitcher | Roger Clemens |
| Outfielder | Ken Griffey, Jr. | Pitcher | Goose Gossage |
| Outfielder | Kirby Puckett | Pitcher | Dennis Eckersley |
| Catcher | Carlton Fisk | Manager | Tony LaRussa |

*"This isn't a guy that shows up at season openers to take bows and get his picture in the paper and has to have his secretary of state tell him where first base is. This man knows baseball."*

— Sportswriter Dick Young in the *New York Daily News*

1945 — House Speaker Sam Rayburn throws out the first ball of the last season to commence during World War II. The Senators wore black armbands in respect for Franklin D. Roosevelt, who had recently died. The band on manager Ossie Bleuge's uniform is plainly seen. A young Lyndon Johnson is visible in the first row and an aging Walter Johnson can be seen between Rayburn and Bleuge.

# ACKNOWLEDGMENTS

Thomas B. Koetting of *The Wichita Eagle* for his superbly reported story of May 3, 1992, disclosing that Dwight Eisenhower, before and during his West Point days, played professional baseball under a pseudonym.

Hank Thomas, grandson of Walter Johnson, for sharing with us the voluminous research he has compiled on his grandfather for a forthcoming biography of the great pitcher.

The staff of the National Baseball Library at Cooperstown, New York, who have got to be the best in the business of specialized information.

Bob Davids, founder of the Society for American Baseball Research, for his carefully documented list of games attended by presidents.

The text and photo archivists at the Hoover, Franklin D. Roosevelt, Truman, Eisenhower, Kennedy, Johnson, Nixon, Ford, Carter and Reagan presidential libraries.

Kevin Cartwright and Olivia S. Anastasiadis of the Richard Nixon Library and Birthplace, Yorba Linda, California, for sharing information about the Nixon Library's exhibit "America's Presidents and America's Pastime."

Frank J. Aucella of the Woodrow Wilson House
Bob Brown of the Baltimore Orioles
Mary Corliss of the Museum of Modern Art Film Still Archives
Raymond V. Curiale
Brigg Hewitt
George Hobart, the Library of Congress
Dave Kelly, Library of Congress sports specialist
Bobby Kraft
Norbert Kraich, before, during and after his Society for American Baseball Research directorship
Nancy Jo Leachman, librarian of Society for American Baseball Research
Ron Menchine for access to his remarkable collection of baseballiana
Kenneth B. Miller
The Prints and Photographs Department, the Library of Congress
Michael T. Sheehan, director of the Woodrow Wilson House
Bob Staples
Phil Wood of WTEM Radio, Washington, D.C.
Gail Zimcosky of Cleveland State University

# BIBLIOGRAPHY

Addie, Bob. "Presidential Pitch Began with Taft," *The Sporting News*, April 15, 1967.

Alexander, Charles C. *Ty Cobb*. New York: Oxford University Press, 1984.

Allen, Charles F., and Jonathan Portis. *The Life and Career of Bill Clinton, the Comeback Kid*. New York: Birch Lane Press, 1992.

Allen, Lee. *Cooperstown Corner: Columns from The Sporting News, 1962-1969*. Cleveland: Society for American Baseball Research, 1990.

Allen, Mel, and Frank Graham, Jr. *It Takes Heart*. New York: Harper and Brothers, 1959.

Alvarez, Mark. *The Old Ball Game*. Alexandria, Virginia: Redefinition, 1990.

Andreano, Ralph. *No Joy in Mudville: The Dilemma of Major League Baseball*. Cambridge, Mass.: Schenkman, 1965.

Asinof, Eliot. *Eight Men Out*. New York: Ace Books, 1963.

Bakst, M. Charles. "Talkin' baseball — For George Bush, memories of the Babe and the summer game warm the chill of winter," *The Providence Sunday Journal*, March 3, 1985.

Barber, Red. *1947—When All Hell Broke Loose in Baseball*. New York: Doubleday, 1982.

Bartlett, Arthur. *Baseball and Mr. Spalding*. New York: Farrar, Strauss and Young, 1951.

Bealle, Morris A. *The Washington Senators*. Washington: Columbia Publishing Co., 1947.

Benson, Michael. *Ballparks of North America*. Jefferson, N.C.: McFarland, 1989.

Blackwell's Durham Tobacco Co. *The Bull Durham Baseball Guide, Volume 2*. New York: 1911.

Boswell, Tom. "A President's Passion for Baseball," *The Washington Post*, March 31, 1989.

Boswell, Tom. *How Life Imitates the World Series*. Garden City, New York: Doubleday, 1982.

Bragdon, Henry Wilkinson. *Woodrow Wilson: The Academic Years*. Cambridge: The Belknap Press of Harvard University Press, 1967.

Brady, Dave. "Dave Powers: 'Mr. Baseball' in White House," *The Sporting News*, May 25, 1963.

Brady, Dave. "JFK Goes All the Way With Nats — as Laotian Prince Cools Heels," *The Sporting News*, April 18, 1962.

Brondfield, Jerry. *Hank Aaron ... 714 and Beyond*. New York: Scholastic Books, 1974.

Burr, Harold C. "The Sport of Presidents," *Baseball*, June 1939.

Carmichael, John P., et al. *My Greatest Day in Baseball*. New York: Tempo, 1968.

Carruth, Gorton, and Eugene Ehrlich. *The Harper Book of American Quotations*. New York: Harper & Row, 1988.

Chadwick, Henry. *DeWitt's Base-Ball Guide for 1874*. New York: Robert M. DeWitt, Publisher, 1874.

Chieger, Bob. *The Cubbies: Quotations on the Chicago Cubs*. New York: Atheneum, 1987.

Chieger, Bob. *Voices of Baseball: Quotations on the Summer Game*. New York: Atheneum, 1983.

Cochrane, Gordon S. *Baseball: The Fan's Game*. New York: Funk & Wagnalls, 1939.

Coffin, Tristram Potter. *The Old Ball Game: Baseball in Folklore and Fiction*. New York: Herder and Herder, 1971.

Cohen, Marvin. *Baseball the Beautiful*. New York: Links Books, 1974.

Cohen, Richard M., David S. Neft and Roland T. Johnson. *The World Series*. New York: The Dial Press, 1976.

Couzens, Gerald Secor. *A Baseball Album*. New York: Lippincott and Crowell, 1980.

Craig, Roger, with Vern Plagenhoef. *Inside Pitch*. Grand Rapids, Mich.: Eerdsman Publishing, 1984.

Creamer, Robert W. *Babe: The Legend Comes to Life*. New York: Simon and Schuster, 1974.

Creamer, Robert W. *Stengel: His Life and Times.* New York: Simon and Schuster, 1984.

Crepeau, Richard C. *Baseball: America's Diamond Mind 1919-1941.* Orlando, Florida: University of Central Florida, 1980.

Daniel, Daniel M. "Roosevelt Saved Baseball With His 1942 Letter to Judge Landis," *Baseball,* June 1945.

Day, Laraine. *Day with the Giants.* Garden City, N.Y.: Doubleday, 1952.

Deford, Frank. "Spring Has Sprung," *Sports Illustrated,* April 10, 1978.

Deming, Richard. *Vida.* New York: Lancer, 1972.

Dickson, Paul. *Baseball's Greatest Quotations.* New York: HarperCollins, 1991.

Dickson, Paul. *The Dickson Baseball Dictionary.* New York: Facts on File, 1989.

Dowd, Maureen. "Bush Takes Mubarak Out to the Ball Game," *The New York Times,* April 4, 1989.

Durocher, Leo, with Ed Linn. *Nice Guys Finish Last: Sport and American Life.* New York: Simon and Schuster, 1975.

Durso, Joseph. *Baseball and the American Dream.* St. Louis: *The Sporting News,* 1986.

Durso, Joseph. *Casey.* Englewood Cliffs, N.J.: Prentice-Hall, 1967.

Einstein, Charles. *The Fireside Book of Baseball.* New York: Simon and Schuster, three volumes, 1956, 1962, 1968.

Einstein, Charles. *Willie's Time.* New York: J.P. Lippincott, 1979.

Feller, Bob. *Strikeout Story.* New York: Bantam, 1948.

Fleming, G.H. *The Unforgettable Season.* New York: Penguin, 1981.

Ford, Whitey, with Phil Pepe. *Slick.* New York: Dell, 1987.

Frank, Stanley. "Baseball's Biggest Day," *The Saturday Evening Post,* April 12, 1952.

Freehan, Bill. *Behind the Mask.* Cleveland: World, 1970.

Frick, Ford C. *Games, Asterisks, and People.* New York: Crown, 1973.

Frommer, Harvey. *New York City Baseball.* New York: Macmillan, 1980.

Frommer, Harvey. *Rickey and Robinson.* New York: Macmillan, 1982.

Garagiola, Joe. *Baseball Is a Funny Game.* New York: Bantam Books, 1962.

Gardner, Martin. *The Annotated Casey at the Bat.* New York: Bramhall House, 1967.

Gibson, Bob, with Phil Pepe. *From Ghetto to Glory.* New York: Popular Library, 1968.

Goldstein, Warren. *Playing for Keeps: A History of Early Baseball.* Ithaca: Cornell University Press, 1989.

Gordon, Peter, with Sydney Waller and Paul Weinman. *Diamonds Are Forever.* San Francisco: Chronicle Books, 1987.

Graham, Frank, and Dick Hyman. *Baseball Wit and Wisdom.* New York: David McKay, 1962.

Graham, Frank. *Baseball Extra.* New York: A.S. Barnes, 1954.

Grey, Zane. *The Shortstop.* New York: Grosset and Dunlap, 1937, reprint of 1909 original.

Griffith, Clark, as told to A. E. Hotcher. "Presidents Who Have Pitched for Me," *This Week,* April 10, 1955.

Hano, Arnold. *A Day in the Bleachers.* New York: Crowell, 1955.

Hano, Arnold. *Willie Mays.* New York: Grosset and Dunlap, 1966.

Hartt, Rollin Lynde. "The National Game," *The Atlantic,* August 1908.

Hawkins, Burton. "The Season's Opener is the Game for Presidents," *The Sunday Star Pictorial Magazine,* April 13, 1947.

Higgins, George V. *The Progress of the Seasons.* New York: Henry Holt, 1989.

Hill, Art. *I Don't Care If I Never Come Back.* New York: Simon and Schuster, New York, 1980.

Hollander, Zander. *Presidents in Sport.* New York: Associated Features Inc., 1962.

Hudson, Mary Ann. "Decades of Bipartisan Support," *The Los Angeles Times,* July 7, 1992.

Hynd, Noel. *The Giants of the Polo Grounds.* New York: Doubleday, 1988.

Kerr, Jon. *Calvin: Baseball's Last Dinosaur*. Wm. C. Brown Publishers, 1990.

Koetting, Thomas B. "One Strike On Ike," *The Wichita* (Kansas) *Eagle*, May 3, 1992.

Koppett, Leonard. *A Thinking Man's Guide to Baseball*. New York: Dutton, 1967.

Koufax, Sandy, with Ed Linn. *Koufax*. New York: Viking, 1966.

Kuhn, Bowie. *Hardball*. New York: Times Books, 1987.

Lasorda, Tommy, with David Fisher. *The Artful Dodger*. New York: Avon Books, 1985.

Libby, Bill, and Vida Blue. *Vida: His Own Story*. Englewood Cliffs, N.J.: Prentice-Hall, 1972.

Lieb, Frederick G. *Baseball As I Have Known It*. New York: Tempo, 1977.

Lieb, Fred. *Connie Mack*. New York: G.P. Putnam's Sons, 1945.

Lipsyte, Robert. *SportsWorld*. New York: Times Books, 1975.

Lomax, Stan, and Dave Stanley. *A Treasury of Baseball Humor*. New York: Lantern Press, 1950.

Lowenfish, Lee, and Tony Lupien. The *Imperfect Diamond*. New York: Stein and Day, 1980.

Lowry, Phillip J. *Green Cathedrals*. Cooperstown, N.Y.: Society for American Baseball Research, 1986.

Luciano, Ron and Dave Fisher. *Strike Two*. New York: Bantam Books, 1984.

Macht, Norman L. "Presidents made a pitch for popularity at games," *USA Today Baseball Weekly*, June 29, 1992.

Mack, Connie. *From Sandlot to Big League: Connie Mack's Baseball Book*. New York: Alfred A. Knopf, 1950.

Martelle, Scott. "Women in Diamonds," *The Detroit News*, March 5, 1992.

Masin, Herman L. *Baseball Laughs*. New York: Scholastic Books, 1964.

Mathewson, Christy. *Pitching in a Pinch*. New York: Putnam, 1912.

McCullough, David. *Truman*. New York: Simon & Schuster, 1992.

McGraw, Tug, and Joseph Durso. *Screwball*. Boston: Houghton Mifflin, 1974.

Mead, William B. *Baseball Goes to War*. Washington, D.C.: Farragut Publishing Company, 1985.

Mead, William B. *The Official New York Yankee Hater's Handbook*. New York: Perigee Books, 1983.

Mead, William B. *Two Spectacular Seasons*. New York: Macmillan, 1990.

Mitchell, Gary, with Gary Matthews. *They Call Me Sarge*. Chicago: Bonus Books, 1985.

Mitchell, Jerry. *The Amazing Mets*. New York: Grosset & Dunlap, 1970.

Mungo, Raymond. *Confessions from Left Field*. New York: Dutton, 1983.

Murray, Tom, editor. *Sport Magazine's All-Time All Stars*. New York: Signet, 1977.

Nash, Bruce, and Allan Zullo. *The Baseball Hall of Shame*, volumes 1-4. New York: Pocket Books, 1985, 1986, 1987, 1990.

Nelson, Kevin. *The Greatest Stories Ever Told About Baseball*. New York: Perigee Books, 1986.

Nelson, Kevin. *Baseball's Greatest Quotes*. New York: Simon and Schuster, 1982.

Newman, Bruce. "An All-Around Sportsman in His Own Right," *Washington Star*, December 14, 1978.

Nichols, Edward J. *Historical Dictionary of Baseball Terminology*. Ann Arbor, Mich.: University Microfilms, 1939.

Novak, Michael. *The Joy of Sports*. New York: Basic Books, 1976.

Okrent, Daniel, and Harris Lewine. *The Ultimate Baseball Book*. Boston: Houghton Mifflin, 1979.

Okrent, Daniel and Steve Wulf. *Baseball Anecdotes*. New York: Oxford, 1989.

O'Neill, Thomas P. Jr., with William Novak. *Man Of the House: The Life and Political Memoirs of Speaker Tip O'Neill*. New York: Random House, 1987.

Pepe, Phil. *No-Hitter*. New York: Scholastic Books, 1972.

Pepe, Phil. *The Wit and Wisdom of Yogi Berra.* New York: Hawthorne, 1974.

Peterson, Harold. *The Man Who Invented Baseball.* New York: Scribners, 1973.

Plimpton, George. "A Sportsman Born and Bred," *Sports Illustrated*, December 26, 1989.

Polner, Murray. *Branch Rickey.* New York: Atheneum, 1982.

Quigley, Martin. *The Crooked Pitch: The Curveball in American Baseball History.* Chapel Hill, N.C.: Algonquin Books, 1984.

Reagan, Ronald. *Where's The Rest Of Me.* New York: Karz Publishers, 1981.

Reichler, Joseph L., editor. *The Baseball Encyclopedia.* New York: Macmillan, various editions.

Rice, Grantland. *The Tumult and the Shouting.* New York: A.S. Barnes, 1954.

Richter, Francis C. *The Millennium Plan of Sporting Life.* Philadelphia: Sporting Life Publishing Co., 1888.

Rickey, Branch. *The American Diamond.* New York: Simon and Schuster, Simon and Schuster, New York, 1965.

Rieland, Randy. *The New Professionals.* Alexandria, Va.: Redefinition, 1989.

Ritter, Lawrence S. *The Glory of Their Times.* New York: Macmillan, 1966.

Robbins, Sabin. Untitled paper on Woodrow Wilson and sports, prepared in connection with a show on the subject at the Woodrow Wilson House in Washington, D.C. On file at the Wilson House.

Roberts, Michael. *Fans.* New York: New Republic Books, 1976.

Robinson, Brooks. *Third Base Is My Home.* Waco: Word Books, 1974.

Robinson, Jackie, with Charles Dexter. *Baseball Has Done It.* Philadelphia: J.B. Lippincott, 1964.

Robinson, Jackie, with Alfred Duckett. *I Never Had It Made.* New York: Putnam, 1972.

Rothan, Martin. *New Baseball Rules and Decisions Book.* Lexington, Ky.: Baseball Decisions Co., 1947.

Ruth, George Herman. *Babe Ruth's Own Book of Baseball.* New York: Putnam, 1928.

Ruth, George Herman. *How to Play Baseball.* New York: Cosmopolitan Book Co., 1931.

Ruth, George Herman, with Bob Considine. *The Babe Ruth Story.* New York: Dutton, 1948.

Sale, I. Kirk. "Mr. President Goes to the Ballpark," *Sport*, May 1969.

Schecter, Leonard. *The Jocks.* New York: Paperback Library, 1969.

Schlossberg, Dan. *The Baseball Book of Why.* Middle Village, N.Y.: Jonathan David Publishers, 1984.

Schlossberg, Dan. *The Baseball Catalog.* Middle Village, N.Y.: Jonathan David Publishers, 1980.

Schlossberg, Dan. *Hammerin' Hank.* New York: Stadia Sports Publishing, 1974.

Schwed, Fred Jr. *How to Watch a Baseball Game.* New York: Harper & Brothers, 1957.

Seymour, Harold. *Baseball: The Early Years.* New York: Oxford University Press, 1960.

Seymour, Harold. Baseball: *The Golden Age.* New York: Oxford University Press, 1971.

Seymour, Harold. Baseball: *The People's Game.* New York: Oxford University Press, 1990.

Shea, Thomas P. *Baseball Nicknames.* Hingham, Mass.: Gates-Vincent Publications, 1946.

Smith, Curt. *America's Dizzy Dean.* St. Louis: Bethany, 1978.

Smith, H. Allen. *Low and Inside.* New York: Doubleday, 1949.

Smith, Myron J. *Baseball: A Comprehensive Bibliography.* Jefferson, N.C.: McFarland, 1986.

Smith, Red. "R.S.V.P. to Commissioner Kuhn," *The New York Times*, February 11, 1974.

Smith, Red. *To Absent Friends from Red Smith.* New York: Atheneum, 1982.

Smith, Robert. *Babe Ruth's America.* New York: Thomas Y. Crowell, 1974.

Smith, Robert. *Baseball.* New York: Simon and Schuster, 1947.

Smith, Robert. *Baseball's Hall of Fame.* New York: Bantam, 1965.

Sobel, Ken. *Babe Ruth & the American Dream.* New York: Random House, 1974.

Sperling, Dan. *A Spectator's Guide to Baseball.* New York: Avon Books, 1983.

Spink, J. G. Taylor. *Judge Landis and Twenty-Five Years of Baseball.* New York: Thomas Y. Crowell, 1947.

Stern, Bill. *Bill Stern's Favorite Baseball Stories.* New York: Pocket Books, 1949.

Talese, Gay. "White House Top Right-Hander Warming Up," *The New York Times,* April 13, 1958.

Theoharis, Athan G. and John Stuart Cox. *The Boss.* New York: Bantam Books, 1988.

Thompson, Fresco. *Every Diamond Doesn't Sparkle.* New York: David McKay, 1964.

Turkin, Hy. *The Baseball Almanac.* New York: A.S. Barnes, 1955.

Uecker, Bob, with Mickey Herskowitz. *Catcher in the Wry.* New York: Jove, 1982.

United States Congress, House of Representatives, Committee on the Judiciary. *Organized Baseball.* Washington, D.C.: Government Printing Office, 1952.

Vanderberg, Bob. *Sox: From Lane and Fain to Zisk and Fisk.* Chicago: Chicago Review Press, 1982.

Vecsey, George. *The Baseball Life of Sandy Koufax.* New York: Scholastic Books, 1968.

Vecsey, George. *Joy in Mudville.* New York: McCall, 1970.

Vecsey, George. "The Best of Casey Stengel," *Newsday,* August 31, 1965.

Veeck, Bill, with Ed Linn. *The Hustler's Handbook.* New York: Berkley Books, 1965.

Veeck, Bill. *Veeck—As in Wreck.* New York: New American Library, 1962.

Voight, David Q. *American Baseball.* Norman, Ok.: University of Oklahoma, 1966.

Voight, David Q. *American Through Baseball.* Chicago: Nelson-Hall, 1976.

Vosburgh, John R. "One-Pitch Presidents," *The New York Times Magazine,* April 18, 1948.

Wallop, Douglass. *Baseball: An Informal History.* New York: Norton, 1969.

Wallop, Douglass. *The Year the Yankees Lost the Pennant.* New York: Norton, 1954.

Weaver, Earl. *It's What You Learn After You Know It All That Counts.* New York: Pocket Books, 1969.

Weaver, Earl. *Winning!* New York: William Morrow, 1972.

Whitfield, Shelby. *Kiss It Goodbye.* New York: Abelard-Schuman, 1973.

Williams, Peter. *The Joe Williams Baseball Reader.* Chapel Hill, N.C.: Algonquin, 1989.

Williams, Ted, with John Underwood. *My Turn at Bat.* New York: Simon and Schuster, 1969.

Williams, Ted. *The Science of Hitting.* New York: Simon and Schuster, 1970.

Wills, Maury, with Don Freeman. *How to Steal a Pennant.* New York: Putnam, 1976.

Yastrzemski, Carl, with Al Hirshberg. *Yaz.* New York: Tempo, 1968.

Zoss, Joel, and John Bowman. *Diamonds in The Rough.* New York: Macmillan, 1989.

# INDEX

# W

Wagner, Dick, 149–150
Wagner, Honus, 63, 95
Wallace, Henry, 73, 80
Walsh, Christy, 68
Walter Johnson High School, 109–110
Warner Brothers, 168, 169
Warren, Earl, 106
Washington, George, 3, 7, 8, 14
Washington Nationals, 9
Washington Senators, 4, 11, 14, 20, 24, 27, 34, 35, 38, 44, 46, 47, 48, 50, 51–53, 54, 59, 76, 77, 79, 83, 84, 85, 89, 96, 100–101, 106, 107–112, 118, 120, 123, 127, 130, 137, 142, 144, 175, 187, 190, 194, 211
Washington Touchdown Club, 127
Webb, Del, 107
Weems, Mason, 14
Werber, Bill, 99
Wesleyan University, 36, 38
West Point, 93, 95
White House, 3, 9, 11, 115, 118, 120, 127–128, 130, 151, 168, 170
Whitfield, Shelby, 59
Wilkie, Curtis, 153
William, Edward Bennett, 162
Williams, Joe, 60
Williams, Ted, 59, 108, 110, 118, 127, 142, 171, 179, 202
Willkie, Wendell, 75
Wilson, Edith Galt, 33, 36, 37, 187
Wilson, Woodrow, 4, 28, 31–40, 51, 72, 187
"Winning Team, The," 169–170
Wirtz, Willard, 120
World Series, 34, 35, 47, 51–53, 57, 60, 64–66, 67, 81, 87, 104, 108, 111, 137, 158–159, 170, 174
Wright, George, 11
Wright, Harry, 27
Wrigley, Philip W., 65
Wrigley Field, 166, 168

# Y

Yale University, 171, 172, 175, 176, 178
Yankee Stadium, 10, 44, 61, 67–68, 171
Yastrzemski, Carl, 130, 134
Young, Cy, 25, 109
Young, DeAnn, 158
Young, Dick, 210

# Z

Zad, Marty, 109
Ziegler, Ron, 109, 137

William B. Mead was a bureau manager and Washington correspondent for United Press International, a prize-winning writer for *Money* magazine, and an associate editor of *Washingtonian* magazine. *Baseball: The Presidents' Game* is his seventh book about baseball. A native of St. Louis, he now lives in Bethesda, Maryland.

Paul Dickson is a longtime freelance writer and author of more than thirty books, including *Baseball's Greatest Quotations* and *The Dickson Baseball Dictionary*, winner of the 1989 SABR-Macmillan Baseball Research Award. Born in Yonkers, New York, he now lives in Garrett Park, Maryland.